The Story of

Old Fort Johnson

New York

W. Max Reid

HERITAGE BOOKS
2008

HERITAGE BOOKS
AN IMPRINT OF HERITAGE BOOKS, INC.

Books, CDs, and more—Worldwide

For our listing of thousands of titles see our website
at
www.HeritageBooks.com

Published 2008 by
HERITAGE BOOKS, INC.
Publishing Division
100 Railroad Ave. #104
Westminster, Maryland 21157

Copyright © 1906 W. Max Reid

Other books by the author:
The Mohawk Valley

Illustrated by John Arthur Maney

All rights reserved. No part of this book may be reproduced or transmitted in any form or by any means, electronic or mechanical, including photocopying, recording or by any information storage and retrieval system without written permission from the author, except for the inclusion of brief quotations in a review.

International Standard Book Numbers
Paperbound: 978-0-7884-0889-2
Clothbound: 978-0-7884-8053-9

To

MY RESPECTED FRIEND

MAJOR-GENERAL JOHN WATTS DE PEYSTER

THROUGH WHOSE GENEROSITY

OLD FORT JOHNSON BECAME THE PROPERTY OF THE MONTGOMERY COUNTY

HISTORICAL SOCIETY

THIS BOOK IS LOVINGLY DEDICATED

PREFACE

THE acquisition of the old baronial mansion of Sir William Johnson through the successful efforts of a few members of the Montgomery County Historical Society and the generosity of Maj.-Gen. J. Watts de Peyster, to whom this volume is dedicated, suggested the idea of a short account or history of Old Fort Johnson, as this stone building on the Mohawk has been named. It has been called by various names: Castle Johnson, Mount Johnson, and, lastly, Fort Johnson, each one, in a way, a misnomer.

The few pages of statistics that I had in mind has unaccountably grown to a generous-sized volume, with numerous illustrations by my dear friend and companion in many a delightful outing on stream and plain and in the forest, John Arthur Maney.

The title, *The Story of Old Fort Johnson*, indicates the character and purpose of this work. It is not intended as a history of the life of Sir William Johnson, the grand old man of frontier literary fame, but as I reread the manuscript which is before me, I find that his name dominates nearly every page.

It seems strange that a valley that was and is the highway to the great west, the Gate to India, has not had more attention from historians and writers of fiction, until this, the twentieth century.

It is true that W. L. Stone, Sr., and Col. W. L. Stone, Jr., have given us an authentic history of the valley in *The Life of Joseph Brant* and of *Sir William Johnson* (from both of which books I have quoted freely), but until the advent of Harold Frederic and Robert Chambers, novelists, and of Augustus C. Buell, historian, the valley seems to have been neglected. Augustus C. Buell is dead, but I desire at this time to express my appreciation for many kind words and great assistance from the author of *Sir William Johnson, Paul Jones, William Penn*, and other successful books. He died while his last book, *William Penn* was in the hands of the publisher.

It would be a considerable task to enumerate all of the early writers to whom I am indebted for valuable information in regard to the dates and material used in this volume. It is sufficient to say that every man, be he novelist or historian, who writes a book must take advantage of the researches of others, if he is to give to his readers trustworthy information; and I may close this preface with the remark that a history would be of very little value if all of its pages were evolved from the mind of one individual.

W. M. R.

AMSTERDAM, N. Y., July, 1906.

CONTENTS

	PAGE
CHAPTER I	1

Sir William and his Irish sweetheart—His leave-taking—Arrival in the New World—An account of his boyhood days—Résumé of his life from 1738 to 1774.

CHAPTER II.   19

The domestic affairs at Fort Johnson — Catherine Weisenburg — Caroline Hendrick — Molly Brant — Personality of Sir Wm. Johnson—Fort Johnson fortified—Order of defence.

CHAPTER III.   27

Sir William Johnson at the battle of Lake George.

CHAPTER IV.   39

Pontiac—Devil's Hole—Ambuscade at Bushy Run—Johnson's life threatened—Anger of Mohawks.

CHAPTER V.   54

Vagaries of men's minds—Sir John Johnson.

CHAPTER VI.   69

Mohawks at Oghwaga and Oriskany — Molly Brant driven from Indian castle by the Oneidas — Interview between General Herkimer and Joseph Brant.

CHAPTER VII   91

Old documents found in Glen-Sanders house—Résumé of history of war in the valley of the Mohawk — Diary of Wm. Colbraith at Fort Schuyler — The first raising of the Stars and Stripes over an American Fort.

CHAPTER VIII   100

Capture of Walter N. Butler— Han Yost Schuyler and others— Escape of Butler.

vii

Contents

Chapter IX. 111
Sir John Johnson's second raid 1780 — Battle of Stone Arabia — Battle of Klock's field — British account of the raids of Captain Joseph Brant (Thayendanaga).

Chapter X. 123
Colonel Marinus Willett — Battle of Dorlach (Sharon Springs).

Chapter XI 134
Lady Johnson — Her captivity and escape — Sir John's first raid in 1780 — Recovery of the silver plate and its subsequent destruction — Wounding of Major Stephen Watts.

Chapter XII 149
Will of Sir William Johnson.

Chapter XIII 161
Genealogy of the Johnson family.

Chapter XIV 165
Major-General J. Watts de Peyster, Donor, Philanthropist — De Peyster family — Richmond collection — Hon. Stephen Sanford.

Chapter XV. 174
Land grants : Royal, Kingsborough, Sacandaga.

Chapter XVI. 182
Summer rambles — Schoharie Creek from source to overflow — Skeletons of aborigines — Photographs of forest and lake — A boulder that walked away — Historic characters of Tribes Hill — The historic copper kettle.

Chapter XVII 189
The early Mohawk Indians' idea of the Creation.

Chapter XVIII. 198
Episode at the siege of Fort Schuyler — The murder of the maidens.

Chapter XIX 225
A visit to Dadanascara, the summer home of Alfred de Graff — Charming views and historic scenes thereabout — Ancient Indian camp on the Vrooman farm revisited.

ILLUSTRATIONS

	PAGE
OLD FORT JOHNSON AND THE KAYADEROSSEROS CREEK *Frontispiece*	
THE VALLEY OF THE MOHAWK FROM HIGHLANDS AT HOFFMAN, N. Y.	2
THE GREAT FALLS OF THE MOHAWK, COHOES, N. Y.	6
THE BLUFF BELOW THE FALLS, COHOES, N. Y.	8
OLD FORT JOHNSON IN 1753 Drawn by Col. Guy Johnson.	12
GHOST ROOM AND A GHOSTLY VISION, OLD FORT JOHNSON	16
SIR WILLIAM JOHNSON, BART. From an old print.	22
FORT JOHNSON.—THE GROVE OF LOCUSTS	26
FOOT HILLS OF THE ADIRONDACKS. NEAR THE SACANDAGA	30
UPPER FALLS OF ADRIUTHA	36
THE MOHAWK AT SCHENECTADY	38
THE ISLANDS OF THE MOHAWK. A VISTA FROM "THE ANTLERS"	46
A CORNER IN A CELLAR UNDER OLD FORT JOHNSON	50
SIR JOHN JOHNSON, BART.	56

Illustrations

	PAGE
MIDWINTER IN THE MOHAWK VALLEY	58
DEEP-CASEMENTED WINDOW IN THE LADY JOHNSON ROOM	60
FIREPLACE AND OVEN, GUY PARK	66
CAPTAIN JOSEPH BRANT	72
SKULL AND THIGH-BONES AND BROKEN POTTERY FOUND IN MOUND GRAVE AT FORT HUNTER, N. Y. ALSO COPPER BEADS AND SHELL ORNAMENT FOUND IN INDIAN GRAVE NEAR COXSACKIE, N. Y.	74
JUNCTION OF THE MOHAWK AND SCHOHARIE RIVERS, WITH ERIE CANAL AQUEDUCT	76
A CORNER OF OLD ST. GEORGE'S CHURCHYARD, SCHENECTADY, N. Y.	80
GLEN-SANDERS HOUSE, SCOTIA, N. Y., 1713	84
COL. BARRY ST. LEGER	88
From an old print.	
UPPER ONEGA CREEK	92
OLD MILE-SQUARE ROAD, ONEGA CREEK	98
THE OLD KLOCK HOUSE, ST. JOHNSVILLE, N. Y.—1750	110
ORNAMENTED WINDOW, CHURCH AT STONE ARABIA	114
LADY JOHNSON, "LOVELY POLLY WATTS," WIFE OF SIR JOHN JOHNSON, BART.	132
THE EAST ROOM, OLD FORT JOHNSON	136
THE DOORWAY, OLD FORT JOHNSON	150

Illustrations

	PAGE
A Door at Old Fort Johnson	152
The Hall, Old Fort Johnson	154
Old Fireplace, Guy Park	156
West Room, Old Fort Johnson	158
A Corner of Guy Park	160
Statue of Sir William Johnson, Bart., Johnstown, N. Y.	162
J. Watts de Peyster	166
From a steel engraving.	
Memorial Tablet Erected in Honor of Major-General John Watts de Peyster	168
Part of Richmond Collection of Aboriginal Antiquities	170
Hon. Stephen Sanford	172
An Attic Window, Old Fort Johnson	174
Johnson Hall, Johnstown, N. Y.	176
Cayadutta Creek, Running through the Battlefield of Johnstown	178
The Mohawk in the Chilly Grasp of Winter	180
Mound at Fort Hunter where a Number of Indian Skeletons were Uncovered	182
Great Turtle Pond, Fort Hunter, N. Y.	186

	PAGE
THE JELLES FONDA COPPER KETTLE. A REVOLUTIONARY RELIC	188
THE AUTHOR RESTORING THE GREAT MOHAWK JAR	190
A COLONIAL DOORWAY, GUY PARK	196
WINE VAULT CELLAR, OLD FORT JOHNSON	202
CLUB HOUSE OF "THE ANTLERS."	224
ABANDONED HIGHWAY TO ALBANY, LEADING TO DADANASCARA FORD	228
DADANASCARA GORGE	230

The
Story of Old Fort Johnson

The Story of Old Fort Johnson

CHAPTER I

THE EARLY LIFE OF SIR WILLIAM JOHNSON—HIS IRISH SWEETHEART—RÉSUMÉ OF HIS LIFE FROM 1738 TO 1744

WE call the valley in which we live the Beautiful Mohawk and glory in the varied scenes of beauty that meet our eyes at each successive change of season. When the Ice King has bound river and rivulet in his chilly grasp and the deep azure of running streams has given place to his mantle of white, when the bordering hills, clad no longer in verdure bright, but dotted here and there with patches of sombre green, and whose slopes reflect back to the eye all of the rays of the spectrum combined like a huge cloak of ermine, we marvel at its beauty and are proud of its grandeur.

In the spring, with its budding freshness, and in summer, with its maturity of verdure, we find delight in sunshine and in storm; but autumn, which brings with it thoughts of the dying year, changes the valley into a veritable garden of beauty—not with the sear and yellow leaf of Old England, but with the myriads of shades of green and brown and crimson, and all the innumerable tints of gray and olive.

Rocks, rills, and ravines, hills, valleys, and flat land, vistas of higher grounds, and misty outlines of distant mountains add color and majesty to the distant landscape.

Did you ever pay an extended visit to the level lands of Ohio or the rolling plains of the prairie lands of the far western States?

And when, on your return, you struck the narrows of the Mohawk Valley at Little Falls and at the Nose, did not your heart swell with pride as you quoted in a whisper—for you dare not trust your voice—

> Breathes there the man with soul so dead
> Who never to himself hath said,
> "This is my own, my native land"?

Into this valley in all its pristine loveliness came William Johnson, in the leafy month of June, 1738.

In the county of Meath, Ireland, and on the upper waters of the river Boyne, whose outlet forms the Bay of Drogheda and whose shores in the eighth century gave foothold to the Scandinavian pirates, is the small village of Smithtown, the birthplace of Sir William Johnson. Not many miles away, but across the border of the adjoining county of Down, lies the estate of the family of Sir Peter Warren and called Warrentown, the home of the mother of Sir William.

At the dawn of a beautiful day in the autumn of 1737, a young man, whose every motion gave evi-

The Valley of the Mohawk from Highlands at Hoffman, N. Y.

dence of vigorous manhood, with grace of movement and strength of limb, was striding along a country highway leading to the port town of Drogheda.

The gray of dawn barely disclosed the flitting forms of trees whose bare trunks rose in small clusters from the bogs on each side of the road. The young man walked with long, swinging strides, switching his high top-boots with a riding whip at every step. As the gray of the horizon gave way to the crimson and gold of the perfect morning, it disclosed the bright colors of the garments of the traveller. His straight and vigorous limbs were seen to be encased in buff knickerbockers and high top-boots, while his broad shoulders and well-turned arms were clothed in the green coat and long buff waistcoat frequently worn by the Irish gentlemen of the eighteenth century.

The hat that adorned his head was of conical shape, with broad band ornamented with a polished silver buckle of large size in front, and on the lapel of his coat was a bow of orange ribbon.

The sun rising above the bleak moor disclosed the handsome features of a young man of twenty-three, whose dark gray eyes and full crimson lips broke into a happy smile as he espied the drooping form of a comely girl leaning on a stile constructed in a break in the hawthorn hedge which formed a border to the road he was travelling.

Pale and trembling, and with eyes disclosing the agony of grief and a long night's vigil, the young maiden swiftly approached the young man, and with the abandon of perfect love flung herself into his outstretched arms, exclaiming: "O Will, my darling, I cannot, cannot let you go; take me, oh, take me with you! do not leave me to die, as I surely will if I am left alone with my grief." Pressing her yielding form close to his breast, and arresting her frantic words with a long, clinging kiss, he replied, with intense fervor in his voice: "Ah, mavourneen, do not grieve so, do not look upon this as a final parting. It is true that America is a long way from dear old Ireland, and the wilderness will be dreary without your dear presence, but if there is a way of reaching its distant shores there is also a way of returning. Cheer up, my darling: through the kindness of dear old Uncle Peter I am to be placed in a way to make my fortune and a home for us two in this grand New World, to which so many are hastening.

"Think of the happiness to come, when I am rich enough to build a home and then return for you, my love. What will the terrors of the forest lands amount to, when, with a home for you and me, we will be safe and happy from the stern edicts of parental authority? Kiss me, my love, and give me God-speed and a cheerful good-bye."

Stifling her tears she raised her eyes to his, and with one hand on his breast, clasped closely in his own, and with the other pointing to the golden disk of the sun whose rounded edge was illuming the dreary moorland, she said:

"Will, as surely as that sun will rise and at the close of day sink from sight in the west, so surely are you going out of my life in your voyage to the western world—but not out of my heart, love, not out of my breaking heart. Kiss me, dear, I hope that your dreams will prove true."

He clasped her in his arms again, protesting that he would prove true to his Irish lass and that he would build a home for her in the forest lands of the beautiful Mohawk. Gently disengaging herself from his strong arms, with a smile on her lips more expressive of grief than her tear-laden eyes, she leaned against the stile as she watched his form disappear in the distance. Then, with arms outstretched toward the sea, she exclaimed in an agonizing whisper, "Oh, my sweetheart, my darling, will never come back to me; never come back!" and sank unconscious on the dew-laden turf at her feet.

We know not the name of this maiden; we know not the reason why Sir Peter Warren offered the superintendence of his lands on the Mohawk River to his nephew, William Johnson. All that we are told is that, on account of an unfortunate love affair, he was induced by his uncle to emigrate to America.

Very little has been written of the boyhood of William Johnson, but the late Augustus C. Buel, a descendant of Sir William by one of the daughters of Caroline, his first Indian wife, has given us some facts not hitherto printed.

It is said that he was the son of Christopher Johnson and Anna Warren, a sister of Admiral Warren. Christopher Johnson may have been a school teacher in his younger days, but from 1692 to 1708 he was an officer in a cavalry regiment then known as Cadogan's Horse.

At the time his son William was born (1715), he was a local magistrate for Carlingford. It is said that he was a "cripple," as the result of a wound from a French bullet received at Oudenarde.

In May, 1726, Admiral Peter Warren wrote in his diary: "Visiting me Mistress Nancy (Anna) Johnson with her Young Son, William, aged eleven. William is a Spritely Boy, well grown, of good parts, Keen Wit but most Onruly and Streperous. I see in him the Makings of a Strong Man. Shall keep my Wether Eye on this lad."

From the little that we can learn of his school days it would seem as though the opinion of·his Uncle Peter, that he was most unruly and "Streperous," was correct. His family wished to make a soldier of him, but he declared against this scheme and announced that he wished to become a barrister. He grew rapidly, but the development of his body seems to have outrun that of his mind, and his school days at the Academy ended suddenly in expulsion. It seems that an attempt on the part of the moderator to chastise young William resulted in failure on the part of the instructor, and the haling of the lad before a magistrate on a charge of assault and battery, who was fined seven guineas and "put on the limits" for twenty-one days, followed by a flagellation from his crippled father upon his return home.

For the next three or four years he studied law with a barrister named Byrne and was listed for examination in the spring of 1737, but a month or two before the assizes met he received an offer from

The Great Falls of the Mohawk, Cohoes, N. Y.

Sir William Johnson

his uncle Peter to go to America and take charge of a large tract of land, consisting of 14,000 acres situated in the Mohawk Valley and now known as the town of Florida, N. Y.

Late in the summer of 1737 he sailed for America, arriving in New York in December. The young man spent the winter in New York as guest of his aunt, Sir Peter Warren's wife.

Lady Warren was a daughter of Stephen De Lancey, one of the richest merchants in New York, whose family held leadership in the most refined and aristocratic society of the provincial metropolis. It was in this social environment William passed the winter, and it is said that "he bore himself with tact, dignity, and grace worthy of wider experience and maturer years"; during which period he met many influential men and women whose interest and influence were vastly useful to him in later years.

Although young Johnson was not knighted until about eighteen years later, in order to save confusion I will in future pages speak of him as Sir William, a title by which he is so well known in history.

We have seen that Sir William came in contact with men of influence in the affairs of the colony, particularly the De Lanceys. Hon. James De Lancey, a brother of Lady Warren, was commander-in-chief of the province of New York, and Lieut.-Governor in 1754, '55, '57, and became a firm friend of Sir William.

Although his school days ended somewhat disastrously, the months he spent in the law office of barrister Byrne prepared him for the various duties he was called upon to perform as land agent for various persons on both sides of the Atlantic; and although, perhaps, the diction of his letters to the Lords of the Board of Trade does not compare very favorably with those of Secretary John Pownell and others, his letters were models of good reasoning and rare judgment, and his suggestions in regard to the conduct of his affairs as Indian Commissioner received the utmost consideration of that august body and were generally adopted.

In most of the stories of the life of Sir William Johnson the early years of his sojourn in the valley are disposed of in a very few words, and even then the writers show a lamentable ignorance of the geography of the valley.

Some content themselves by stating that he built a trader's store west of Schenectady, and others locate his headquarters near Fort Hunter. W. L. Stone's statement would naturally convey that impression.

The facts are that the location selected by Sir William for his storehouse and dwelling was about half a mile east of the Mohawk River bridge at Amsterdam, on the south side, his nearest neighbors at that time being Alexander and Hamilton Phillips about two miles farther east, and Philip Groat on the opposite or north side of the river at Adriutha or Cranesville. In time other buildings were erected, until the place was dignified with the name of "Johnson's Settlement." It was so called during the Revolution and as late as 1795. Somewhat later, or after the construction of the Erie Canal, a Roman

The Bluff below the Falls, Cohoes, N. Y.

Sir William Johnson

Catholic chapel was erected there or in that vicinity, which was the beginning of the immense parish of St. Mary's Roman Catholic Church of Amsterdam, N. Y.

Here Sir William lived for five years, when he moved into the large stone house at Akin which he called Mount Johnson until 1755, when the place was surrounded by a palisade and renamed Fort Johnson.

While living on the south side Johnson diligently worked to improve and develop the large estate of his uncle Sir Peter Warren, who desired to keep its 14,000 acres intact by renting sections of the lands to tenants on long leases. Sir William, however, early found that such a scheme was impracticable, and with the consent of his uncle soon sold a large portion of it in farms of 150 to 300 acres.

(W. L. Stone quotes a letter from Sir Peter to Sir William in which is this sentence, "My love to Mick." He says: "This name occurs twice, but I do not know who Mick is." It was probably Michael Byrne, who somewhat later was closely connected with Johnson, and whose son married one of Sir William Johnson's daughters by his Indian wife Caroline.)

It is said that the rude storehouse and dwelling were completed in 1738, and a housekeeper secured of Lewis Phillips in the person of a young Dutch girl whose services the said Phillips had secured by paying fifteen pounds due the captain of the ship that brought her across the Atlantic, as passage money. At the suggestion of Phillips, Sir William paid his friend the fifteen pounds and took the girl. This girl, whose name was Catherine Weisenburg, afterward became the mother of his son John and his two daughters Anna and Mary, and at some subsequent period, the exact date of which is not known, was married to William Johnson by the Rev. James Barclay, missionary of Queen Anne's Chapel at Fort Hunter.

Very soon after Sir William had erected his buildings at "Johnson's Settlement" he purchased land on the north side of the Mohawk River on both sides of the Kayaderoseros or Old Fort Creek, for the purpose of erecting a grist-mill. In 1742 the mill was erected, and also the substantial stone building now known as Fort Johnson.

The thought has often come to me, for whom did he build this stone structure? Was it for his servant Catherine, or was it to be a home for his sweetheart in old Ireland?

Suffice it to say that Mount Johnson, as it was then called, was constructed in a style that in those days may well have been termed magnificent, and even to this day bears the impress of the brand of an experienced architect. Here his daughters Anna and Mary were born and here his first wife, Catherine, died. His son, known after Sir William's death as Sir John Johnson, was born at the "Johnson Settlement," on the south side.

It was while living in this grim, gray stone mansion that nearly all of the notable events of this notable man's strenuous life transpired.

It was here that his two daughters received their

Sir William Johnson

educational instruction from governesses, and were married. Here also he installed King Hendrick's niece Caroline as companion, by whom he had three children, two daughters who married white men, and one son, the half-breed Teg-che-un-to or William of Canajoharie, mentioned in Sir William's will. It was in this building in 1752 that Caroline died and was succeeded by Molly Brant, the majority of whose children were born here.

In 1746 Johnson was made Indian Commissioner, having by kindness and tact obtained almost complete control of the warlike Iroquois. One of the historians of the valley says:

> The distinguishing feature of Sir William Johnson's character was strict integrity. In this is to be found the great secret of his marvellous ascendency over the Indians. Cajoled and cheated by the English traders and land agents for a long series of years, the Amerind had learned to regard the name of Englishman as a synonym of fraud and deceit. From the time, however, of the Baronet's settlement in the valley of the Mohawk until his decease, they had ever found him true to his word and conscientious in his dealings.
>
> Another trait of Sir William's character—and which added not a little to his influence over the Indians—was his power of adaptation. This he possessed in a remarkable degree. He was at ease whether entertaining in his baronial mansion on the Mohawk the polished scion of nobility, or the rude savage; whether mingling in the salons of wealth and fashion, or seated on the earthy floor of a bark wigwam. The same facility of action was shown in all his varied relations. A trader in peltry, he was upright and affable; a counsellor, he was sagacious and prudent; a major-general, courageous but cautious; superintendent of Indian affairs, wise and discerning; a baronet of the realm, courtly in his hospi-

talities; a large landed proprietor with a numerous tenantry, kind and just.

Somewhat later, through the jealousy of Governor Shirley, he was constrained, in order to sustain his dignity and honor, to resign his office of Indian Commissioner, but the Iroquois were so aroused and so vociferous in their demand for his reinstatement that he was reappointed with almost unlimited powers.

The old stone house during the French and Indian war was the scene of great activity. This was the headquarters of the militia of the valley, over which Sir William was commandant, and which in May, 1756, he led to German Flats to check the advance of the French, who were said to be marching down the valley. It proved to be a false alarm. In June, an Indian runner brought news that a large force of French and Indians was organizing on the Canadian border for a raid through the valley. One section of this body of troops was directed to kill or capture Sir William and to destroy Fort Johnson and all property in its vicinity. It was during this period of unrest that the old building was fortified by a palisade and the name changed from Mount Johnson to Fort Johnson.

Notwithstanding the jealousy and enmity of Governor Shirley, Captain General of the provinces of New York and New England, he appointed Sir William Johnson Major General and commandant of four thousand troops raised in the above provinces for the purpose of capturing Crown Point, a French fortress on Lake Champlain.

Old Fort Johnson in 1753.
(Drawn by Col. Guy Johnson.)

Sir William Johnson

The story of the battle of Lake George, as it is called, has been so often told that I will not attempt to describe it at this time, although it seems to me as though the denizens of the Mohawk Valley deserve more than a passing credit for that victory. In the first place Major General Johnson, the commandant, was a resident of this section of the valley. In June, 1755, more than eleven hundred Indians were in camp on the flats in front of old Fort Johnson, not three miles west of the city of Amsterdam. Of this number three hundred were warriors equipped for war; the balance consisted of women and children, gathered here to subsist on the bounty of Sir William while their warlike sons and husbands followed their friend to victory.

It must, indeed, have been a picturesque sight. Imagine a motley array of Indian families around hundreds of camp-fires extending along the flats east and west for a mile or more; women cooking their food while the kids foraged far and near; painted warriors lounging on the ground in graceful attitudes; sachems and chiefs thronging the halls of the building in consultation with Sir William, whose word was law unto them; the octogenraian King Hendrick, his large form grown stout and unwieldy, striding majestically to and fro, his ample blanket covering his gorgeous attire, his broad, heavy face seamed by age and further disfigured by broad bands of black and vermilion.

On June 27, 1755, Sir William wrote to Governor De Lancey:

I am working with the sachems and leading men from

morning until night. The fatigue I have undergone has been too much for me. It still continues and I am scarcely able to support it. I am distressed where to get victuals for such numbers; they have destroyed every green thing upon my estate and destroyed all my meadows. But I must humor them at this critical juncture.

In 1760-61 the last French war, as it is called, ceased. At this period of comparative peace Sir William Johnson, having secured entire control of the Kingsboro Patent of twenty-six thousand acres in the vicinity of the present town of Johnstown, turned his attention to the improvement of that estate, it having become more valuable and important than his smaller estate at Fort Johnson. Here he built a commodious mansion and gave it the name of Johnson Hall. This was completed in 1763 and Sir William moved into it in the early spring, leaving Fort Johnson and the lands adjoining in possession of John Johnson, his eldest son, who continued to occupy it until the death of his father, July 11, 1774.

Except the trouble arising out of the Pontiac war, which was practically crushed in 1763 although Pontiac did not smoke the calumet of peace with Sir William until July 23, 1766, the Baronet's life was comparatively free from the hardships and turmoils which marked the two decades of his residence on the Mohawk River. In fact, treaties then made with all the Indian tribes practically ended his direct personal attention to Indian affairs, and he only retained under his personal supervision the faithful Mohawks, Oneidas, Oghwagas, and Tuscaroras, his three deputy superintendents, George Crogan, Daniel

Ghost Room and a Ghostly Vision, Old Fort Johnson.

Claus, and Guy Johnson, relieving him of the care of the "far Indians."

At Johnson Hall, Johnstown, Sir William died, as he lived—in harness—after a long speech to about six hundred Indians, mostly Iroquois, who had assembled at Johnson Hall to invoke his influence to prevent the invasion of the Indian country on the Ohio, known as Dunmore's war.

He was at this time much weakened by a chronic disease, and the excessive mental effort and exposure to an extremely hot sun brought on prostration, which culminated in cerebral apoplexy, from which he died in about two hours. Sir John Johnson was at his home, Fort Johnson, when his father was prostrated,—ten miles from Johnson Hall.

Young William Johnson—the half-breed son (Teg-che-un-to)—mounting a blooded horse from Sir William's racing stable, reached Sir John with the news at five oclock in the afternoon, although the horse he rode was ruined. Sir John instantly mounted his own best steeple-chaser and covered nine miles of the distance in thirty minutes; but the horse fell dead within a mile of Johnson Hall, and Sir John borrowed a horse from a farmer and soon arrived at his father's bedside. But his father was unconscious and in a few minutes ceased to live.

Of Sir John's life at Fort Johnson we know but little. It is said that he was just twenty-one years old when Sir William moved to Johnson Hall and left him in charge of the Fort. In early life he wooed, won, but did not wed a very pretty girl of good family, named Miss Clara Putnam, by whom he had a son and a daughter. Miss Putnam was keeping house for him at the old Fort Johnson mansion when, on June 29, 1773, he married Miss Mary Watts of New York city, a woman noted for her great beauty and accomplishments, but before Sir John returned from New York he caused Miss Putnam and her children to be sent across the river into the town of Florida. Late in life he gave her money, and a house and lot in Schenectady, where she died about the year 1840.

The first tenant of Fort Johnson, after Sir John fled to Canada and Lady Johnson was held as hostage at Albany was Albert Vedder, the founder of the city of Amsterdam, 1779. In 1800 the property belonged to Jacob C. and John C. Cuyler. The successive purchasers were as follows:

Jeremiah Schuyler, February 22, 1817;
John J. Van Schaick, January 8, 1820;
George Maxwell, December 14, 1824;
George Smith, January 26, 1826.

George Smith died intestate and the property was divided into nine parcels and all sold between 1836 and 1844.

Fort Johnson mansion and lands adjoining were purchased by Dr. Oliver Davidson who afterward sold the same premises to Almarin Young, from whom they were purchased by Ethan Akin. While living at Fort Johnson, Dr. Davidson's daughter wrote the well-known poem entitled "The Sale of Old Bachelors."

It would indeed be strange if tradition did not point to a tragedy connected with this old building. In

Sir William Johnson 17

the early part of the nineteenth century a country store stood where Mr. Shepard's residence stands, on the corner east of the creek. Tradition says that one night a drunken fellow whose name was Joe Burke entered the store and got into a fight with the storekeeper, punishing him severely, and then fled pursued, by the angry merchant with a gun. The merchant followed him into Fort Johnson and saw him pass up the stairs toward the attic. Just as Burke reached the attic stairs his pursuer fired and killed him, his blood spattering the stair-casing. Subsequently the body was removed to the cellar, placed in a cask of whiskey in one of the wine vaults constructed in the foundations of the large chimneys, until the ice broke up in the spring, when it was rolled to the river and sent floating on its way to the sea. The matter was hushed up, and is only known now by tradition.

Of course there is a ghost room, but the ghost seems to have been a very mild character.

In preparing this chapter, it has been my desire to make plain to you the very prominent part that Fort Johnson played in the early history of the valley and to establish the claim made that this grim, gray stone mansion is entitled to the designation of the first baronial mansion in New York State.

After the battle of Lake George Sir William was notified (November 11, 1755) that King George II. had conferred upon him the dignity of baronet of the realm of Great Britain and also a gift of $20,000 as a reward.

Thus you see that Sir William was not only created a baronet before he had secured the Kingsboro grant of 26,000 acres and while Johnstown was yet a wilderness, but for eight years after he was knighted and entitled to the title of Sir William he resided at Fort Johnson.

In studying the life of Sir William Johnson in the light of the twentieth century, my mind frequently reverts to the heart-broken Irish lass, lying on the dew-laden turf, in the dawn of the summer morning so long ago. How true was her prophecy—her lover never came back.

CHAPTER II

THE DOMESTIC AFFAIRS OF SIR WILLIAM AT FORT JOHNSON

THE domestic affairs of Sir William Johnson have received a great deal of criticism from the historians of the valley, and the intemperate zeal of some of them in putting in type racy bits of gossip of doubtful authenticity, that floated around the valley a half-century after his death, would have made them in this century good yellow journalists.

These stories have marred the character of an otherwise great man. His first wife, Catherine Weisenburg, seems to have been a handsome, companionable girl, with whom he was unavoidably brought into close relation through the exigencies of a forest life, at a time when the custom of bundling was not considered a heinous crime by the old Dutch families who were his neighbors. (See Professor Pearson's *Schenectady Patent*, p. 366.)

The poor girl, far from home and relatives, practically a slave for a term of years, perhaps did not until after years consider her relations with Sir William as unlawful or sinful, and should not be mercilessly condemned when the situation is thoroughly understood. That Sir William married her soon after the birth of his children indicates a desire to atone as far as was in his power for the social sin they had committed.

Soon after her death, and at a time when his influence over the Iroquois was being made manifest, he took to his home the daughter of Chief Abraham, who was also a niece of King Hendrick, the most powerful chief of the tribe of Mohawks. She became his Indian wife by the laws and usages of the Indians, and I have always thought that the selection was made as a matter of policy, in order to please the Mohawks, who had nominally made him a chief. Caroline was her English name.

This occurred in 1747. By Sir William she had two daughters and a son: the daughters were named Charlotte and Caroline, and the son was called William, for his father. He was the first born and is the "William Johnson *alias* Teg-che-un-to" who is mentioned in his will as William of Canajoharie. In 1753 Caroline died in childbirth at the birth of her second daughter, who was also named Caroline.

This gives us approximately the date of the installation of Molly Brant as Sir William's second Indian wife, or housekeeper, as she has been variously called, which was subsequent to that date and probably soon after the death of Caroline Hendrick, as she is sometimes called.

As Molly Brant was her niece it would seem as though she must have been a frequent visitor to her aunt and well known to Sir William, as the daughters were adopted by her as her own, and lived with her at Fort Johnson, while William, the half-breed boy, was brought up by his grandfather Abraham or his uncle

Domestic Affairs

"Little Abe," at Canajoharie Castle at Danube, New York.

William Johnson (Teg-che-un-to) the half-breed was educated by Sir William at Dr. Wheelock's school at Lebanon, Conn., and was killed by the Oneida half-breed Thomas Spencer at the battle of Oriskany.

Molly Brant, who was a sister of Thayendanega (Joseph Brant), was about sixteen years old when her aunt Caroline died, in 1753, and lived at Fort Johnson and Johnson Hall until Sir William's death in 1774, a period of about twenty years, during which time she had eight children.

There is nothing that is recorded about this picturesque character who came into Sir William's life accidentally, we might say, to lead us to suppose that the unique union of this strong, forceful man with the handsome and intelligent though unlettered maiden of the forest was not in every way a union of affection and fidelity, unto death.

During the Revolutionary period and subsequent to that time she and her half-breeds, with the exception, probably, of Peter, her eldest-born, seem to have reverted to savage impulses, tempered somewhat by the civilizing education of twenty years' life in a family who associated with the foremost people in the colonies.

What seems very strange is the fact that she does not appear to have taken an exalted station in the new settlements of the Caniengas or Mohawks on the shores of Grand River and at Deseronto in Canada. The fact is that with the exception of the date of her death (1805) she appears to have dropped out of the pages of history entirely after her flight to Niagara in 1779.

Reverting to the daughters Charlotte and Caroline: Charlotte, the eldest, married a young British officer shortly before the Revolution, but who afterward joined the Continental army and fell at Monmouth Court-House. His name was Henry Randall. They had two children, one named Charlotte Randall, who married George King. George and Charlotte King had a daughter Charlotte, who was the grandmother of my informant.

The other daughter of Molly Brant's predecessor (Caroline), whose name was also Caroline, married a man named Michael Byrne, a clerk in Sir William's office of Indian affairs. Byrne was killed at Oriskany in Butler's Rangers. His young widow, Caroline Johnson, went with the Brants to Canada and afterward married an Indian agent named MacKim, whose descendants are still living in Canada.

A description of Sir William is given by Mrs. Julia Grant, an artist who painted his portrait in 1751:

A little scant of six feet—five feet eleven and one-half inches—neck massive, shoulders broad, chest deep and full, limbs large and showing every sign of great physical strength. Head large and finely shaped. Countenance open, frank and always beaming with good nature and humor—a real Irishman as he is for Irish wit. Eyes large, a sort of black-gray, or grayish black. Hair with a tinge of auburn in certain lights. In conversation he is a most delightful person.

His mode of living is that of an English gentleman at his country seat, and I was astonished to find on this remote frontier, almost in the shade of primeval forests, a table

Sir William Johnson, Bart.
From an old print.

loaded with delicacies and Madeiras, ports and Burgundies of the rarest vintage. His table is seldom without guests, and his hospitality is a byword the region round.

During my stay he had Indian chiefs to dine with him several times. Their attire was the same as white people's and for the most part they conversed in English. This disappointed me, because I wished to sit at table with genuine Indians in blankets and leggings and talking nothing but gibberish through an interpreter. Among those I met at Colonel Johnson's table were the venerable and noble-looking old chief Hendrick, now over seventy years of age; his brother Abraham, about sixty years of age, chief of a Mohawk clan and father of Caroline the beautiful young Indian woman who was mistress of the household; also Nicklaus Brant, chief of the Upper Castle of the Mohawks, a man of most prodigious silence and the most grave and solemn courtesy.

Colonel Johnson is the soul of method. He must have fifty or sixty people in his employ besides the negroes, and he oversees everything they do. Marvellous! And then he attends to a mass of complicated public business besides!

The different names that have been applied to the baronial mansion of the Mohawk are somewhat confusing and somewhat misleading. We hear it called Mount Johnson, Castle Johnson, and Fort Johnson.

When it was erected (in 1742) Sir William named it Mount Johnson, which was a misnomer, as it was built on a flat, and the hills in its vicinity could not by any stretch of imagination be called mountains. At the time of its construction, or soon after, the mansion as it now stands, and which has been described elsewhere, was flanked to the east and to the west by two low stone buildings used respectively for kitchen and servants' quarters. A little to the south and in front of the servants' quarters was a structure of stone, two stories high, used as a store. Until 1755 this collection of buildings was called Mount Johnson.

At the date named a feeling of unrest and insecurity led Sir William to fortify his home by erecting a stockade around it, said stockade being made of palisades sharpened at one end and set firmly in the ground closely together and reinforced by long timbers spiked horizontally to the palisades, binding the whole firmly together. Each of the four corners was fortified by a bastion. In the curtain on the south side was a gate heavily ironed. Judging from the distance given from the river bank to the south curtain, the stockade was not more than sixty feet from the stone mansion which it protected. No trace of this wooden fortification is visible at the present time. A picture made by Guy Johnson previous to 1755 shows a small guard-house situated on the slope of a hill about one third of the distance from the top. This hill is on the east or left bank of the Old Fort Creek, one hundred and fifty paces from the stone building.

The following order, copied by a Colonel T. Bailey Meyers from the original, will give an idea of the care taken by Sir William for the protection of his home during that period of the French war embraced between 1755 and 1761. The order is addressed to Lieutenant Alexander Turnbull, Aug. 9, 1756.

FORT JOHNSON.

1st. You will keep your Party sober and in good order and prevent their having any unnecessary Intercourse with the Indians lest any difference might arise between them from too much familiarity.

2d. If any difference should arise between them, if the

Domestic Affairs

Indians use any of your party ill, I am to be immediately acquainted with it.

3d. The Sergeant to take care that the Men's Quarters be kept very Clean and that they wash well and freshen their Salt Provisions, the neglect of which makes them subject to many Disorders.

4th. You will in the daytime keep one Sentry on the Eminence to the Northward of the House, who upon seeing the enemy advance is to fire his piece and retreat to the fort. Another Sentry to be posted at the Gate of the Fort on the outside, who is also to enter the Fort on the advanced Sentry alarming him.

5th. When there are no Indians here the Gates to be locked at 8 o'clock in ye evening and opened at six in the morning, first looking around about to see that all is safe and clear, the advanced Sentry then to be posted every Day.

6th. Whenever an alarm is given by the advanced Sentry, you will order three Patteroes [or Peæroes, a very small kind of cannon] immediately to be fired, that being the signal I have given to the Mohawks, and on their approach near the Fort, when challenged, they are to answer "George" as distinct as they can, then to be admitted if practicable.

7th. In case of any attack the 2 Bastions to be properly manned and the 2 curtains also, there mixing some of my People with yours. The remainder of my People to man the Dwelling House and fight from thence, making use of the Four Wall Pieces and Musquetoons and of the windows fitted for them.

The men's arms and ammunition to be kept in Good Order.
    I am Sir
      Yrs.,
        Wm. Johnson.

There is another account, by a traveller who is said to have visited Fort Johnson in 1757, which differs somewhat from the foregoing description and which I am now satisfied is incorrect. He says that the building had port-holes and a parapet. For parapet we should read stockade. Port-holes in the building there were none.

In Sir William's order to Lieutenant Turnbull he says: "The remainder of my People to man the Dwelling House and fight from thence, making use of the Four Wall Pieces [a small cannon] and Musquetoons *and of the windows prepared for them.*" The house is two stories high, with a large attic in which are four dormer windows with sash opening outward. In the heavy sill of each of these windows is a round hole a little to the left of the centre. These holes are about one and a half inches in diameter and were undoubtedly used for the pivot of the small *cannon* spoken of, and were probably taken for port-holes by the traveller. The walls are intact and show no evidence of any holes having been made in them for the purpose of firing either guns or cannon.

Fort Johnson.—The Grove of Locusts.

CHAPTER III

SIR WILLIAM JOHNSON AT THE "BATTLE OF LAKE GEORGE"

LAKE George, nestling among the foot-hills of the Adirondacks, may well be called historic water, as around its shores have surged warriors, savage and civilized, in conflict, perhaps for ages. The Mahicans, the Adirondacks, Montagnies, and other Algonquin tribes of Canada, the Hurons, and the Mohawks and other Iroquois tribes fought each other along its shores and on its waters for centuries before the advent of the white man upon the continent. Champlain knew of its existence in 1609, when he, together with the Hurons, met and defeated the Mohawks on the shores of the lake that bears his name. It is said that Champlain visited its shores in 1613, being the first white man who gazed upon its waters.

Its Indian name was Andiatarocte, but it was known to the French of Canada, in connection with its larger sister (Lake Champlain), as Lake Iroquois. Cooper calls it Lake Horicon, a corruption of the word Iroquois. In 1645 Father Isaac Jogues paddled its length in a canoe with his Huron guides, on the eve of Corpus Christi, or the "feast of God," and in honor of that feast named it Lac St. Sacrement. This name it retained until 1755, when it was changed to Lake

George by General William Johnson, in honor of King George the Second.

Being separated from the Hudson River by the Luzerne Mountain, the Indian trail from Canada to the Mohawk Valley passed over the level plain to the Great Carrying Place on the Hudson River, and thence down that river, or overland to the early Mohawk castles above Hoffman's Ferry. This plain is also historic ground. Across its surface the Agniers (Mohawks) passed to seek a new home in the valley of the Mohawk, when driven from the St. Lawrence by their savage kindred. Here they fought their neighbors the Mahicans, and after gaining strength recrossed this plain, and in 1609 unexpectedly met defeat at the hands of Champlain on the shores of Lake Iroquois, and on account of that defeat became the deadly enemies of the French colonists. Repeatedly they paddled across these waters carrying death and destruction to the Hurons, whom they utterly destroyed on the shores of Lake Huron in 1649. Across this beautiful lake passed Father Isaac Jogues and Rene Goupil as prisoners in 1642, and again in 1646 Jogues and Lalande, as missionaries, to meet a shameful death on the shore of the Mohawk. In February, 1666, De Courcelles and Tracy with 600 men, and again in October of the same year with 1200 French and Indians, and two pieces of artillery, in a flotilla of bateaux sailed its waters. In 1667 it was the route of Fathers Perrion and Bruyas as missionaries to the Mohawks' country, and on Sept. 8, 1755, it witnessed the conflict known in history as the battle of Lake George, between the English and colonists,

Battle of Lake George

under General Wm. Johnson, General Lyman, and others, and the French forces under Baron Dieskau.

Francis Parkman has told the story of this battle in his usual interesting way, and I have taken the liberty of giving a condensed account of his narrative:

The "last French war" was at its height, and to defeat a contemplated raid on Albany, by the way of Lake Champlain and Lake George, an expedition was organized whose object was the capture of Crown Point, at the upper end of Lake Champlain proper, then in possession of the French. Levies were made on the Eastern States, and Connecticut had voted 1200 men, New Hampshire 500, Rhode Island 400, while New York promised 800, and William Johnson had gathered 1100 Indians, men, women, and children, at his own house, known as Fort Johnson, on the Mohawk River.

This army of raw recruits gathered at Albany preparatory to proceeding to Crown Point by the way of Hudson River to the Great Carrying Place, as it was called, at Fort Edward. The American army numbered about 3000, and the French army, under Baron Dieskau, had reached Crown Point with 3500 regulars, Canadians, and Indians, mostly of the Caughnawaga tribe, from the banks of the St. Lawrence.

The Caughnawagas were composed of converts to the Roman Catholic religion from the Iroquois and other Indians, who, through the influence of the Jesuit priests, had migrated to Canada and formed a settlement on the St. Lawrence River at Lachine Rapids, which was called St. François Xavier du Sault, or St.

Francis Xavier "at the rapids." This name was afterward changed to Caughnawaga, which means in the Iroquois tongue "at the rapids."

Among the followers of General Johnson were four hundred Iroquois, mostly Mohawks, under King Hendrick, who although deadly enemies of the French were loath to fight against their kindred.

Parkman says: "The soldiers were no soldiers, but farmers and farmers' sons who had volunteered for the summer campaign. A greater part brought their own guns but had no bayonets. Most of them carried hatchets in their belts as a sort of substitute, while at their sides were slung powder-horns."

After a tedious wait on the Albany flats the body moved up the Hudson to the Great Carrying Place, where General Lyman had begun a fortified storehouse, which his men called Fort Lyman, but which was afterward named Fort Edward.

Two Indian trails led from this point, one by the way of Wood Creek to Lake Champlain, the other over the plain to Lake George, which last was selected as the route. Two thousand men were ordered to the lake, preceded by axemen to hew out the way. At last they reached their destination. "The most beautiful lake in America lay before them, then more beautiful than now, in the wild charm of untrodden mountains and virgin forests."

The men made a camp near the water, at the head or south end of the lake.

It will be remembered that the Hudson River, only nine miles away, flows south to New York Bay, while

Foot Hills of the Adirondacks. Near the Sacandaga.

Battle of Lake George 31

the waters of Lake George and Lake Champlain flow north to the St. Lawrence.

It would seem that General Johnson intended to advance on Crown Point through Lake George by bateaux, which were constantly arriving on heavy Dutch wagons over the carrying place from Fort Lyman, fourteen miles away to the south. In front of the camp was a forest of pitch pine, on their right was a swamp, on their left the low hill on which Fort George was afterward built, and at their rear the lake. Little was done to clear the forest in front, though it would give excellent cover to the enemy. About three hundred Mohawks were in camp, and were considered great nuisances by the New Englanders.

While Johnson lay at Lake George, Dieskau prepared a surprise for him, and concluded not to wait to be attacked, but moved nearly his whole force to Carrillon, or Fort Ticonderoga, which commanded both routes by which Johnson could advance, that of Wood Creek and that of Lake George. Hearing from a prisoner, who had invented a falsehood, that the English had fallen back, and that there were only five hundred men at Fort Lyman, Dieskau resolved by a rapid movement to seize the place. At noon the same day, leaving part of his force at Ticonderoga, he embarked the rest in canoes and advanced along the narrow prolongation of Lake Champlain that stretched southward through the wilderness to where the town of Whitehall now stands. He came to a point where the lake dwindled to a mere canal, while two mighty rocks capped with stunted forests faced each other from the opposing banks. As they neared the site of Whitehall they turned to the right and entered the lonely lake called South Bay, where they left their canoes and began their march through the forests toward Fort Lyman (Fort Edward). Having captured some mutinous drivers who had left the English camp without orders, they learned that a large force lay encamped at the lake. The Indians having refused to advance to attack the fort, Dieskau resolved to attack the camp at Lake George. Advancing through the gorge they were following, they passed around the south end of French Mountain. When within three miles from the head of the lake a prisoner was brought in who told them that a column of English troops was approaching. Dieskau's preparations were quickly made. The Canadians and Indians moved to the front and hid themselves in the forests along the slopes of West Mountain and the thickets on the other side. Behind every bush or tree crouched a Canadian or an Indian with gun cocked and ears intent, listening for the tramp of the approaching column.

Some of the drivers who had escaped capture returned to Johnson's camp about midnight and reported a war party on the road to Fort Lyman. Johnson called a council at once, and it was determined to send out two detachments of five hundred men each, one toward Fort Lyman and the other toward South Bay. Hendrick, chief of the Mohawks, a brave and sagacious warrior, expressed his dissent after a fashion of his own. He picked up a stick and broke it; then he picked up several sticks and showed that together they could not be broken. The hint was taken, and the two detachments were joined in one. Still King Hendrick shook his head: "If they are to be killed," he said, "they are too many; if they are to fight, they are too few." Nevertheless he resolved to share their fortunes. He was too old and fat to go afoot, but Johnson lent him a horse, which he bestrode, and was soon at the head of the column, followed by two hundred of his warriors. Lieutenant Colonel Whiting soon came up with the balance of the detachment and the whole moved on together, so little conscious of danger that no scouts were thrown out in front or flank, and in full security entered the fatal snare. Before they were completely involved, the sharp eye of old Hendrick detected some sign of an enemy. At that instant a gun was fired from the bushes, the thickets blazed out a deadly fire, and the men fell by scores. Hendrick's horse was shot down and the chief was killed by a bayonet thrust as he tried to rise. Colonel Williams was also killed as he charged up the slopes on the right, calling his men to follow. The rear hurried forward to support their comrades, when a hot fire opened upon them from the forest, and then there was a panic. The van became the rear and the enemy rushed upon it shouting and screeching. After a moment of total confusion a part of Williams' regiment, under command of Whiting, rallied and covered the retreat, fighting behind trees like Indians, and firing and falling back by turns, bravely aided by some of the Mohawks and by a detachment which Johnson sent to their aid. "And a very handsome retreat they made, and so continued till they came within three quarters of a mile of our camp." So ended the fray long known in New England fireside story as the "bloody morning scout."

When the rattle of musketry was heard at the camp, gradually becoming louder, it was known that their comrades were retreating, and hasty preparations were made for defending the camp. A barricade was made along the front, partly by wagons and inverted boats, but chiefly by trunks of trees hastily hewn down in the forest and laid end to end in a row. Three cannons were planted to sweep the road and another was dragged to the ridge of the hill. Five hundred men were detailed to guard the flanks, already protected by swamps, right and left. The rest stood behind the wagons, or lay flat behind the logs and inverted bateaux. Besides Indians (about 300), the force numbered between sixteen and seventeen hundred rustics.

They were hardly at their posts when they saw ranks of white-coated soldiers moving down the road, and the glint of bayonets that seemed innumerable. At the same time a burst of war-whoops rose along the front, and "the Canadians and Indians came running with undoubted courage right down the hill upon us expecting us to flee. If Dieskau had made an assault at that instant, there could be but little doubt of the result. He had his regulars well in hand, but the rest, red and white, were scattered through the woods and swamps yelling and firing from behind trees." The regulars, who deployed and fired by platoons, were met by a fire of grape from the artillery, which broke their ranks and scattered them through

Battle of Lake George

the forest seeking cover. The fire now became general, during which Johnson received a flesh wound in the thigh and returned to his tent, leaving General Lyman in command for the rest of the day. Baron Dieskau was also wounded three times, the last time across the hips, but seated behind a tree he denounced the Canadians and Indians, and ordered his adjutant to lead the regulars in a last effort against the English. But it was too late. Johnson's men were already crossing their row of logs, and in a few moments the whole dashed forward with a shout, falling upon the enemy with hatchets and the butts of their guns. The French and their allies fled.

It may be apropos to introduce at this time the following letter from Baron Dieskau to M. de Vaudreuil:

Camp of the English Army
At Lake St. Sacrement, Sept. 15, 1755.

Sir:

I am defeated; my detachment is routed; a number of men killed and thirty or forty are prisoners, as I am told. I and M. Burnier, my Aid de Camp, are among the latter. I have received my share, four gunshot wounds, one of which is mortal. I owe this misfortune to the Iroquois. [Caughnawagas.] Our affair was well begun, but as soon as the Iroquois perceived some Mohawks, they came to a dead halt; the Abenaquis and other Indians continued some time but disappeared by degrees; this disheartened the Canadians, so I found myself with the French troops engaged alone. I bore the attack, believing that I might rally the Canadians and perhaps the Indians, in which I did not succeed.

The Regulars received the whole of the enemy's fire and were almost cut to pieces. I prophesied to you Sir that the Iroquois would play some scurvy trick; it is unfortunate that

I am such a good prophet; I cannot too much acknowledge Mr. de Johnson's kindness and attention to me. He is to send me to Orange to-morrow. I know not my fate either as regards my health or the disposition of my person.

I have the honor to be &c.,

BARON DE DIESKAU.

Sometime before the final rout several hundred Canadians and Indians left the field and returned to the scene of the morning ambush to plunder and scalp the dead. While resting themselves near a pool in the forest they were set upon by a scouting party from Fort Lyman, chiefly backwoodsmen, under command of Captains Folsom and McGinnis. The assailants were greatly outnumbered, but after a hard fight the Canadians and Indians fled. The bodies of the slain were thrown into the pool which bears to this day the name of Bloody Pond.

The English loss in killed, wounded, and missing at the battle of Lake George was 262, and that of the French, by their own account, was 228. For this victory General Johnson was made Baronet by King George II., and Parliament gave him five thousand pounds.

The expedition of General Johnson and his occupation of the lake led to the building of Fort William Henry, which was located near the lake and east of the two swamps between which Johnson had met and defeated the French under Dieskau. It would seem to have been a rude affair of no very great strength, but strong enough to resist the feeble attempts that were made to capture it between 1755 and 1757, when Montcalm, fresh from his victory at Oswego, advanced against it with 10,000 men, consisting of regulars,

Upper Falls of Adriutha.

Battle of Lake George

Canadians and Indians. Fort William Henry was garrisoned with 2200, under command of Lieutenant Colonel Monroe, a brave Scotch veteran.

Montcalm set out from Ticonderoga the 1st of August, 1757, having sent a detachment to advance along the west side of the lake, while the balance embarked in bateaux and canoes from Burned Camp. The whole force numbered 7600 effective whites and Indians. Parkman says:

> And now, as evening drew near, was seen one of those wild pageantries of war which Lake George has often witnessed. A restless multitude of birch canoes, filled with naked painted savages, glided by shores and islands like troops of swimming waterfowl. Two hundred and fifty bateaux came next, moved by sail or oar, some bearing the Canadian militia and some the battalions of old France, in trim and gay attire; then the cannon and mortars, each on a platform sustained by two bateaux lashed side by side; then the provision bateaux and the field hospital, and lastly a rear guard of regulars.

Montcalm chose for the site of his operations the ground now covered by the village of Caldwell.

We will pass by the story of the siege and assault, the brave defence of Monroe and his little band of heroes and their anxious watching for reinforcements from General Webb, the despair when it became known that Webb had refused to march to their relief, and the final surrender of the gallant defenders, and the massacre of the sick and wounded and a large number of the helpless captives, and the final burning of the heaps of slain, who were placed inside of the fort, which was then set on fire and destroyed.

In July, 1758, General Abercrombie's army, about fifteen thousand strong, sailed down the lake in one thousand boats and attacked Ticonderoga, without success. In July, 1759, General Amherst, with almost an equal force, also traversed the lake, and took Crown Point and Ticonderoga.

General Burgoyne, before he began his march to Saratoga, made this point a depot of his supplies.

There are also stories of Captain Rogers and his rangers that are as interesting as the most lurid tales of romance of the present; of Ethan Allen and his Green Mountain Boys, and other expeditions of the war of the Revolution; and as late as the war of 1814 warlike bodies passed over its placid waters on expeditions of conflict and death to British soldiers, at Cumberland and Plattsburg, on Lake Champlain.

The Mohawk at Schenectady.

CHAPTER IV

PONTIAC—MOHAWKS REFUSE TO JOIN PONTIAC'S INDIANS—THE AMBUSCADE AT BUSHY RUN—THE MASSACRE AT DEVIL'S HOLE—SIR WILLIAM JOHNSON'S LIFE THREATENED—ANGER OF THE MOHAWKS

PONTIAC—what visions of horror and bloodthirsty cruelty are evolved in the mind at the mention of that savage name—massacre, treachery, the vanishing of households, flames, the scalping knife, the wail of infants, the despairing courage of men, the devoted sacrifice of women. Even after a century and a half it chills the blood and arouses murderous thought of retaliation against the fiendish savages that wrought such widespread desolation, and deluged the western and southern frontiers of civilization in blood and ashes.

Francis Parkman, whose interesting histories impress one with careful research and painstaking accuracy, has recorded in detail the destruction of many of the frontier forts and the heroism of their defenders.

He tells how in 1760 Major Rodgers, an English officer, was sent into the country of Pontiac to drive the French out. He met Pontiac and told him his errand and delivered to him several belts of wampum. Pontiac replied, "I stand in the path you travel until to-morrow." This the officer understood to mean that he was not to march further without his leave. The next day Pontiac assured him that he might pass through his country and he would protect him and his party. In this manner the wily chief completely deceived the English by professions of friendship until he had united his tribes and arranged his system of warfare. He appointed a commissary, and issued bills of credit, all of which he carefully redeemed. These bills were made of birch bark, on which was drawn the article wanted, with the figure of an otter, the insignia of the Ottawas.

He relates how the fort at Michillimackinack was captured. It is said that four hundred Indians gathered in the vicinity with presumably friendly intent. On June 4th, the Indians, as if for amusement, began to play ball. Such was the exciting character of the game that many of the soldiers went out to see it. Suddenly the ball was thrown over the stockade as if by accident, and the Indians rushing for it completely surprised the garrison and took the fort. Seventy of the soldiers were butchered and the other twenty reserved for slavery.

Within fifteen days, Pontiac was in possession of all the western garrisons except three, Detroit alone remaining in the distant region of the Northwest.

The garrison of Detroit consisted of three hundred men under Major Gladwin. When Pontiac came, which was before the news of the massacre at Michillimackinack had reached the fort, his warriors, intermixed with many women and children, brought so many articles of trade that suspicion was lulled.

Pontiac

Pontiac encamped some distance from the fort and sent word to Major Gladwin that he had come to trade and wished to hold a talk with him to "brighten the chain of peace" between the English and the Indians. The Major readily consented and the next morning was fixed for the conference.

The same evening, when the fort was cleared of strangers a young and comely Indian woman was found loitering, and being asked what she wanted made no reply. The Major, having noticed her presence in the fort, directed her to be conducted to him. Upon being questioned her answers were confused and constrained as though through fear. The Major talked with her kindly and urged her to tell what she knew, as he would protect her from all harm. Thus assured she told him that the chiefs who were to meet him in council the next morning had formed a plan to murder him and the garrison, and capture the fort; that each chief would come to the council with his gun under his blanket, and when Pontiac gave the signal, which was the delivery to the Major of a belt of wampum, they were to begin their work. Having confidence in the tale of the young girl he at once took every precaution to put the garrison in the best possible state of defence.

At the appointed hour of ten o'clock the next morning Pontiac and his chiefs and a train of warriors filed into the fort, the gates of which were quietly closed and securely guarded. Soldiers were lounging in groups here and there, but did not wander far from their carefully loaded firearms placed near at hand While some were drilling on the parade ground the vigilant eye of the chief evidently noticed an unusual activity among the garrison, but his fears were somewhat quieted by being told that the men were exercising.

The council opened and Pontiac began his speech, but when he came to the signal of presenting the belt, the peculiar attitudes of the men and officers, with guns in readiness and hand on sword told the chief that his plot was discovered. The belt was not given, and Pontiac closed his speech with many professions of good-will to the English. Major Gladwin, however, reproached the chief with his treachery and told him that he knew the whole of his diabolical plot. The Indian made an effort to deny that he intended any injury to his English friends, when the Major stepped to the side of one of the chiefs, pulled aside his blanket, and disclosed the loaded weapon. Pontiac and his warriors were then ordered to leave the fort. The next day began the siege of Fort Detroit, which lasted for twelve months. Sallies were made and frequent attempts of rescue by land and water resulted in many men being killed on both sides.

During this period, Fort Pitt (now known as Pittsburg, Pa.) was closely besieged by a large body of Delawares, Shawnees, and Indians from the Northwest. Although the fort was not strong, it was only garrisoned by a small number of troops under Captain Huger, and was the refuge place for many homeless women and children from the marauding Indians. A body of troops under Colonel Bouquet was sent to the assistance of the place.

Proceeding by forced marches, he gained the valley of Bushy Run. The defiles appeared free. But on the 5th of August, 1763, they were assailed by swarms of Indians who surrounded them on all sides in this narrow passage. The Indian mode of fighting gave them great advantage in this woody country, and the end of the day found Bouquet's troops still in possession of their camp, but the horses of their large convoy were stampeded, and many of the brave soldiers killed and a large number wounded. As the Indians retired when the darkness of night fell around them, the Colonel barricaded his camp and protected his wounded with sacks of flour and other material of which the convoy was composed. The troops, especially the wounded, suffered terribly from the absence of water, of which not a drop could be had.

In the morning the savages again surrounded the camp at a distance of about five hundred yards, their shouts and yells showing that the cordon was complete, and they made several bold efforts to penetrate the camp, and though repeatedly repulsed, could not be drawn close enough to allow the English to use the bayonet.

At last Colonel Bouquet executed a manœuvre which accomplished the desired purpose. Two companies were withdrawn to the interior of the camp, leaving a thin line of soldiers in front. Other companies were ordered to make a short detour through the wood to the right and left. The Indians observing only a thin line in front of them, and thinking that the further movement of troops in the rear indicated a retreat of the English, rushed headlong towards the weak spot, pouring in a heavy and galling fire. As the Indians neared the camp of the wounded, the Highlanders who had gone to the right came round upon the flank of the assailants and fired a close volley into the midst of the crowd, and then with yells as wild as their own fell on them with the bayonet, killing many and putting the rest to flight. But as they turned to run they were met by the two companies of hardy frontiersmen, who charged them from the left, poured among them a second volley, completing the rout. The four companies, uniting, drove the flying savages through the woods, giving them no time to rally or reload their empty rifles, killing many and scattering the rest in hopeless confusion.

Litters were soon made for the wounded, and, the flour and camp equipage being destroyed for the want of horses, the troops moved on in the direction of Fort Pitt. At their first camp they were again attacked, but their assailants received such a warm welcome from the hardy woodsmen that they soon retired. The next day they renewed their march to Fort Pitt, where they arrived on the 10th of August, 1763.

Looking back from the standpoint of the twentieth century, however, we can reflect calmly on the cause and effect of that awful "conspiracy of Pontiac" and give credit to that rude and untutored savage, whose sagacious mind saw in the advance of the English, after the defeat of the French and the conquest of Canada, the gradual extinction of his people.

Pontiac seems to have been a born leader of men, a skilful strategist and fearless warrior. Although we cannot refrain from condemning his methods of warfare, we can appreciate his lofty, savage patriotism. With the skill of a practised diplomat he aroused to fury the savage tribes of the West and cemented them together for the salvation of their country against the advance of the English, who were slowly but surely driving them towards and beyond the Mississippi.

The Ottawa Confederacy, so called, was composed of many western tribes, the chief of which were the Wyandots or Hurons, Pottawatomies, Ojibwas, and Ottawas. Pontiac, although closely identified with the Ottawas, was by birth a Chippewa or Ojibwa. But Pontiac's influence extended farther than the Ottawa Confederacy and included the Delawares, Susquehannocks, Shawnees, and a large portion of the Senecas of western New York.

At that time (1763) the English frontier did not extend beyond the Alleghanies, and, in the province of New York, the German Flats, on the Mohawk. A portion of the Senecas openly espoused the cause of Pontiac, but the Mohawks, Onondagas, Oneidas, and Cayugas indignantly rejected the overtures made by the rebellious westerners. Sir William Johnson's influence, however, prevented some of the Senecas from joining Pontiac's forces, but a large majority could not be restrained. "Had the Six Nations gone over to the side of Pontiac, all the horrors that the French war had witnessed on the borders of New England would have been renewed with even greater ferocity in the province of New York; while with the convoys cut off, and the reinforcements waylaid and killed in passing from Albany to Oswego, Detroit must inevitably have succumbed to the savage."

At this critical period in the history of the province of New York, Sir William Johnson came to the front and placed a firm hand on the Iroquois. He had discovered that the Senecas had sent belts of wampum to the tribes of the Northwest, inviting the Wyandots in conjunction with the Delawares and Shawnees to fall treacherously upon Niagara and Fort Pitt.

Under these circumstances Johnson set out on a wearisome journey through forest, stream, and lake to Detroit, to hold a general Indian council. At Niagara he called a council of the Senecas. He told them about the discovery of their plot, and asked the meaning of such conduct. They replied, denying all knowledge of such a conspiracy, and put on an air of innocent surprise at the accusation. But Sir William was not in the mild mood he commonly used when dealing with the Indians. He had gained their respect and affection by his kindness, and now, when he thundered forth with righteous indignation, they quailed before him.

"As this is so villainous an affair" said he, "and carried so far, I must tell you plainly that I look upon what you now tell me as only an evasion and a kind of excuse to blind us. And I tell you that all the excuses you can make, and all the rhetoric your nation is the master of, will not satisfy the General, nor convince me of your innocence unless a deputation of your chiefs appear at the general council which I am now calling at Detroit, and there, in the presence of all the nations, declare your innocence and disapprobation of what has been done by the two messengers last

The Islands of the Mohawk. A Vista from "The Antlers."

at Detroit. This I expect you will do to show your brethren your innocence, and all the Indians your detestation of so vile a plot." Sir William then returned the belt which they had given with their denial, to show them that he did not believe what they said. This staggered the Indians and they consulted together for some time. At last they declared that they would send the belt to their nation with Johnson's request and had no doubt that some of the chief men would attend the meeting at Detroit.

In due time Johnson met the Indians at Detroit and with the firing of two cannon the great council opened. An immense concourse of savages had gathered from the north, west, and south to see the man at whose house was the council fire of the Six Nations. They were all in gala dress, painted and ornamented. When the council gathered, Sir William and his officers appeared in full uniform. Johnson made them a long, friendly speech, and on the next day the representatives of the Northwest made a satisfactory reply. Kaiaghshota, a Seneca chief, arose, and made an eloquent speech clearing himself and his nation of participating in the recent plot. But Adariaghta, an influential Wyandot brave, sprang to his feet and confronted the Seneca with an exact account of how he had been one of the main plotters, and had been with the messengers sent to the Wyandots by the Senecas. Upon this an Ohio Indian, called the White Mingo, spoke, accusing the Wyandot of endeavoring in his turn to incite the Indians of his locality to a massacre of the English garrisons. A hubbub ensued which was likely to end in blows, when Sir William dissolved the council and the assembly gradually dispersed.

After this Sir William held many councils at Johnstown and the German Flats in order to preserve friendly relations with the Six Nations; otherwise the frontier of New York would have been devastated and all communication with the western parts cut off, but the Senecas continued sullen and rebellious.

In one of his speeches at Johnstown he handed the friendly Iroquois an axe, saying, in regard to the Senecas: "I now deliver you a good English axe, which I desire you will give to the warriors of all your nations, with directions to use it against these covenant-breakers by cutting off the bad links which have sullied the chain of friendship."

Notwithstanding all this the hostile tribes threatened Sir William, and he armed his tenants, numbering some hundred and twenty Highland Scotch families, and fortified his home. The followers of Pontiac were so enraged against Sir William Johnson, whose influence had prevented the Six Nations from joining them, that they swore to take his life. This aroused the faithful Mohawks, who offered to join him against any nation who should attempt to carry such a threat into execution, and eventually led them to join the English in their efforts to suppress the rebellious chiefs. But the Senecas perpetrated one of the most gruesome acts of the war. Parkman thus describes the scene of the awful tragedy called the ambuscade of Devil's Hole. Allusion has been made to the carrying place of Niagara, which formed an essential link in the chain of communication between the province of

New York and the western country. Men and military stores were conveyed in boats up the river Niagara, as far as the present site of Lewiston. Thence a portage road several miles in length, built by Sir William Johnson and finished in 1763, passed along the banks of the stream, and terminated at Fort Schlosser above the cataract. This road traversed a region whose sublime features have gained for it a world-wide renown:

> The river Niagara, a short distance below the cataract, assumes an aspect scarcely less remarkable than that stupendous scene itself. Its channel is formed by a vast ravine, whose sides, now bare and weather-stained, now shaggy with forest trees, rise in cliffs of appalling height and steepness. Along this chasm pour all the waters of the lakes, heaving their furious surges with the power of an ocean and the rage of a mountain torrent. About three miles below the cataract, the precipices which form the eastern wall of the ravine are broken by an abyss of awful blackness, bearing at the present day the name of the Devil's Hole. In its shallowest part, the precipice sinks sheer down to the depth of eighty feet, where it meets a chaotic mass of rocks, descending with an abrupt declivity to unseen depths below, a hundred feet or more. Within the cold and damp recesses of the gulf, a host of forest trees have rooted themselves; and standing on the perilous brink one may look down upon the mingled foliage of ash, poplar, and maple, while, above them all, the spruce and fir shoot their sharp and rigid spires upward into sunlight. The roar of the convulsed river swells heavily on the ear; and far below, its headlong waters, careening into foam, may be discerned through the openings of the matted foliage.

On the 14th of September, 1763, a party of five hundred Senecas lay in wait for a convoy which, having discharged its cargo at Fort Schlosser, was slowly returning escorted by a sergeant and twenty-four soldiers. The party had advanced to that portion of the road which forms the brink of the Devil's Hole. The gulf yawned to their left, while to the right the road was skirted with wooded hills. Suddenly the Senecas rising from their ambush poured a rapid discharge of musketry, and then rushed forward with their glittering scalping-knives to complete their murderous work. Those who escaped the tomahawk were driven over the precipice and with horses and wagons went crashing down among the trees and rocks of the yawning chasm. Three only escaped.

Two companies of soldiers, hearing the firing, hurried to their relief, but being led into ambush shared the same fate, being totally destroyed. The Senecas returned to their homes with eighty scalps.

Again the redoubtable warriors of the "Valley," the terrible Mohawks, saved New York province from destruction, through their loyalty to Sir William. The rebellious western tribes, discouraged with their effort to embroil the whole of the Iroquois in the wholesale butchery of the English, threatened the life of Johnson. At once the Mohawks rallied around him and, with Sir William and Brant as leaders, took up the hatchet against the Ottawa Confederacy. Discouraged at the fact that these fierce warriors not alone remained neutral, but were advancing with the English soldiers intent upon the destruction of the rebellious tribes, many of the western savages withdrew from the support of Pontiac. At a meeting of his chiefs and warriors with Crogan, the courageous deputy of Sir William, Pontiac acknowledged his defeat

A Corner in a Cellar under Old Fort Johnson.

Pontiac

by offering the calumet and belt of peace. Parkman says:

> Crogan's efforts had been attended with signal success. The tribes of the West, of late bristling with defiance and hot for fight, had craved for forgiveness, and proffered the calumet. The war was over; the last flickering of that wide conflagration had died away; but the embers still glowed beneath the ashes, and fuel and breath alone were wanting to rekindle those desolating fires.

In finally making the great peace, Pontiac said: "I now deliver my pipe to be sent to Sir William Johnson, that he may know I have made peace and taken the King of England for my father in presence of all the nations now assembled; and whenever any of these nations go to visit him they may smoke out of it with him in peace."

After Pontiac had sued for peace, some time elapsed before the turbulent tribes ceased their murderous raids. After raising the siege of Fort Pitt the Indians retreated as far as the Muskingum, where they collected their forces and attached new tribes to their confederacy, and made every preparation for renewing the struggle in the spring, but Colonel Bouquet with a large force was sent against them. Unable to check his advance the Delawares, Shawnees, and Senecas asked for a conference to be held on Oct. 18, 1767. Such conference was ordered, and the chiefs and principal warriors of the above tribes were present. The Colonel informed them peace would not be granted unless they should deliver to him all prisoners whom they had held in possession. The Delawares reported 101 prisoners which they would deliver up.

52 The Story of Old Fort Johnson

As many of the raids of the Delawares had been made on the borders of Pennsylvania and the southern frontier of New York an exchange was made at Albany, and is thus described by Mrs. Grant in her *Memoirs of An American Lady:*

The joyful day when the congress was holden for concluding peace I never shall forget. Another memorable day is engraven in indelible characters upon my memory. Madame [Mrs. Schuyler], being deeply interested in the projected exchange, brought about a scheme for having it take place at Albany, which was more central than any other place, and where her influence among the Mohawks could be of use in getting intelligence about the children, and sending messages to those who had adopted them, and who by this time were very unwilling to part with them, in the first place because they thought the children would not be so happy in our manner of life, which appeared to them both constrained and effeminate. This exchange had a large retrospect. For ten years back there had been every now and then, while these Indians were in the French interests, ravages upon the frontiers of the different provinces. In many instances these children had been snatched away while their parents were working in the fields or were afterwards killed.

A certain day was appointed, on which all who had lost their children, or sought those of their relations, were to come to Albany in search of them; where on that day all Indians possessed of white children were to present them. Poor women who had travelled some hundred miles from the back settlements of Pennsylvania and New England appeared here, with anxious looks and aching hearts, not knowing whether their children were alive or how exactly to identify them if they should meet them. I observed these apprehensive and tender mothers were, though poor people, all dressed with peculiar neatness and attention, each wishing the first impression that her child should receive of her might be a favorable one. On a gentle slope near the fort stood a row of temporary huts, built by retainers to the troops; the green before these buildings was the scene of these pathetic recognitions, which I failed not to attend. The joy of even the happy mothers was overpowering, and vented in tears; but not like the bitter tears of those who, after long travel, found not what they sought. It was affecting to see the deep and silent sorrow of Indian women, and of children who knew no other mothers, and clung fondly to their bosoms, from whence they were not torn without the most piercing shrieks; while their own fond mothers were distressed beyond measure at the shyness and aversion with which these long lost objects of their love received their carresses. I shall never forget the grotesque figures and wild looks of these young savages; nor the trembling haste with which their mothers arrayed them in the new clothes they had brought for them, as hoping that with the Indian dress they would throw off their habits and attachments. It was in short a scene impossible to describe but most affecting to behold.

CHAPTER V

VAGARIES OF MEN'S MINDS

IN a conversation with a noted author and soldier in regard to history, particularly American history, he remarked that a true history of the Revolution never had been and probably never would be written. His argument was, that the time to gather historic facts was within the memory of men who participated in a particular episode, and from documents pertaining thereto or from persons living in that period and cognizant of the facts from personal knowledge.

It is true that documentary history is most valuable, but it often tells but a fragment of the story. Personal knowledge is also valuable, but as such history is frequently colored by partisan feeling it often becomes misleading from the interests or personal hatred of the relater, or narrator. Then again, the historian has to depend, in a great measure, on the researches of his predecessors and often finds, if his researches have been thorough, errors made and repeated over and over again by previous writers which make the pages of early history as confusing as the doors of Bagdad marked by Morgianna's chalk. It has been said that the history of one century should be written by the people of the next. This may be

Vagaries of Men's Minds 55

true in a great measure, particularly in biographies and historic episodes of a particular locality.

Distance of time often lends enchantment to the lives of noted or notorious persons, and strips them of the ignominy that pervaded their lives, robing them with motives for their actions that practically array them in a new character. Witness the change of sentiment in regard to Major André, the spy, and the partial rehabilitation of Benedict Arnold. A century after his vile treason we are beginning to think of him as a brave soldier and a great general, and linger over his charge at the battle of Saratoga, his march to Fort Schuyler after the battle of Oriskany, his terrible march to Quebec in November and December, 1775, and his gallantry under the lamented Montgomery at the storming of that northern stronghold.

Even Judas Iscariot is now claimed by some people as a martyr, although still a murderer. They say that it was ordained from the beginning of the world that one of the disciples should betray the Christ and thereby suffer the torments of the damned. A recent writer makes his hero say:

> It is said that Satan entered into Judas, but it looks to me more likely that the Angel of the Lord entered him, he being a good man to start with or our Lord would not have chosen him to be a disciple. Judas knew for sure, after the Lord told him, that one of the disciples would betray the Saviour and go to hell, where the worm dieth not and the fire is not quenched.
>
> Judas loved all of the disciples very much, so he, being imbued with the doctrine of the fatherhood of God and the brotherhood of man, thought that it was his duty to save

the others from the torments of the damned. So he went out and betrayed his Lord for 30 pieces of silver. He knew that if *he* did not do it, it might have been Peter, James or John or some other disciple that the Saviour loved, *because it had to be done by one of them*, for the Lord had said so. After it was done and he knew that the others were saved from the foul deed, he went to the rulers, threw down their money, and went and hanged himself. If he had been a bad man he would have kept the money. Of course Judas knew he would go to hell and Jesus would go to heaven, therefore he (Judas) out of love for his companions committed the deed to save them from torments eternal.

I have been tempted to introduce, at this time, the above incidents or examples, to show the vagaries of men's minds and the tendency of the biographers of this age to analyze the motives of men who have performed great deeds or committed great acts of virtue or villany, and to excuse or rehabilitate the character of historic personages who have been contemned by their cotemporaries.

SIR JOHN JOHNSON

The following is an extract from Maj.-Gen. Watts de Peyster's sketch of Sir John Johnson in his book entitled *The Orderly Book of Sir John Johnson:*

"The Past appeals to the impartiality of the Future. History replies. But often generations pass away ere that reply can be given in a determinate form. For not until passionate pulses have ceased to beat, not until flattery has lost its power to charm, and calumny to vilify, can the verdict of history be pronounced. Then from the clouds of error and prejudice the sun of truth emerges."

Sir John Johnson, Bart.

Sir John Johnson

Sir John Johnson, the son and heir of Sir William Johnson, Bart., was born at Johnson's Settlement, on the Mohawk River opposite the city of Amsterdam, N. Y., November 5, 1742. In the spring following (1743) the family moved into a large stone mansion, which Sir William named Mount Johnson, situated within 200 paces of the confluence of the Kayaderoseros or Old Fort Creek with the Mohawk River. (The place was also called Johnson's Castle.) Here John Johnson grew to early manhood, having the companionship of his younger sisters Anna and Mary, and undoubtedly received the rudiments of education from the governess employed by Sir William for the instruction of his children. (It is said that she was the widow of an English officer, but her name is not known.)

Mrs Grant of Laggan gives a description of the sisters:

These two young ladies inherited in a great measure the personal advantages and strength of understanding for which their father was so distinguished. Their mother dying when they were young bequeathed them to the care of a friend, the widow of an officer who had fallen in battle, who devoted her life to her fair pupils. To these she taught needlework of the most elegant and ingenious kinds, reading, and writing; their monitress not taking the smallest concern in family management, nor the least interest in any worldly thing but themselves; far less did she enquire about the fashions or diversions which prevailed in a world she had renounced upon the death of her husband, and from which she and her pupils seemed to remain forever estranged.

Never was anything so uniform as their dress, their occupations, and the general tenure of their lives. In the morning they rose early, read their prayer-book, I believe, but certainly their bible, fed their birds, tended their flowers, and breakfasted; then they were employed for some hours with unwearied perseverance, at fine needlework for the ornamental parts of dress, which were the fashion of the day, without knowing to what use they were to be put, as they never wore them, and had not at the age of sixteen ever seen a lady(?) excepting each other and their governess; then they read as long as they chose, either romances of the last century [17th] of which their friend had an ample collection, or Rollin's ancient history, the only books they had ever seen; after dinner they regularly, in summer, took a long walk; or an excursion in a sledge, in winter, with their friend, and then returned and resumed their wonted occupations, with the sole variation of a stroll in the garden in summer, and a game of chess, or shuttle-cock in winter.

Their dress was to the full as simple and uniform as everything else; they wore wrappers of the finest chintz, and green silk petticoats; and this the whole year round without variation.

Their hair which was long and beautiful was tied behind with a simple ribbon; a large calash shaded each from the sun, and in the winter they had long fur-lined scarlet mantles that covered them from head to foot.

Their meals were taken apart from the household and their father visited them every day in their apartments. This innocent and uniform life they led till the death of their governess, which happened when the eldest sister Anne was not quite seventeen.

Anne married Col. Daniel Claus and died about 1798. Mary married her cousin, Guy Johnson. She had a daughter Mary, who married Lord Clyde, better known as Sir Colin Campbell, queller of the East India mutiny, and inseparably connected with the siege of Lucknow. You will remember the story: how a small body of British troops under Generals

Midwinter in the Mohawk Valley.

Sir John Johnson

Havelock and Outram were besieged in the residency of Lucknow by ten thousand mutineers. For days and weeks they watched for the coming of relief. At last, when hope is almost gone, a sentry on the walls thinks he hears the pibroch of the Highlanders. With hand to ear he listens with fear and trembling until at last, nearly delirious with joy, he hears the sound again, and shouts to his comrades, "Hark! dinna ye hear the slogan? The Campbells are coming!" and soon the Highlanders under Sir Colin Campbell bring relief to the almost despairing soldiers.

Of Sir John Johnson's early life, I shall have to follow in the footsteps of earlier writers and state that very little is known of his boyhood days. We do know, however, that at the age of thirteen years he and Joseph Brant, then an Indian lad of the same age of John Johnson, followed Sir William's troops to Lake George in 1755 and that Brant is said to have participated in the engagement at "Bloody Pond." Sir John Johnson at the age of seventeen years was present at the fall of Fort Niagara, July 24, 1759. The forces in this engagement were under the command of Gen. Sir William Johnson. In 1761 he accompanied his father to Detroit at a conference with the western Indians, and in 1764 John Johnson, in command of three hundred Iroquois, followed the expedition of Colonel Bradstreet from Fort Niagara to Detroit.

In October, 1765, on the return of Lord Adam Gordon to England after a visit to the Baronet at Johnson Hall, the latter sent his son John with Lord Gordon to England, as he said "to wear off the rusticity of a country education." On being presented at court by such a dignitary, he was at once knighted as the son of Sir William who was afterwards very much gratified on hearing of the fact.

On June 29, 1773, Sir John married the beautiful Mary, affectionately called "Polly," Watts, age nineteen, daughter of John Watts, at his home in New York city. That Sir William did not attend the wedding is proved by the following letter to a friend:

I thank you very kindly for your congratulations on the choice my son has lately made, and am very happy to hear that the young lady appears so deserving in the eyes of my friends, having left it to his own discretion, without tying up his hands in a business on which his future happiness must so greatly depend. The precarious state of my health, however, for some years past, with the often unexpected calls for my presence in the country, put it out of my power to promise myself the pleasure with any certainty of bearing a part on the occasion, notwithstanding the powerful inducements of love and friendship. I am very sensible of the force of both.

On the morning after the ceremony the young couple embarked on a schooner for Albany, reaching Johnson Hall towards the close of July. It is assumed that the happy pair lived at the old baronial mansion, Fort Johnson, where Sir John had been living since 1763, as mentioned in a former chapter. At the death of his father, however, he removed to Johnson Hall, Johnstown.

The death of Sir William was a great blow to his family, and cast a feeling of gloom throughout the length and breadth of the valley of the Mohawk and

Deep Casemented Window in the Lady Johnson Room.

Sir John Johnson

the adjacent territory. For thirty-five years he had been companion, counsellor, and friend of the sturdy Hollanders, thrifty Palatines, volatile Irish, and steady Scotchmen who had peopled the valley and converted gloomy forest lands into smiling meadow-lands within his memory and with his assistance and his advice. His supreme power over those "Indians of Indians," the Iroquois, was an element of safety to them which they were proud to acknowledge and give him full credit for. Owning vast tracts of lands he had become a great factor in the trade and commerce of the valley, and his upright dealing and strict sense of honor had also given to his opinion the force of legal authority in the colonies.

Some historians claim that if he had lived he would have sided with the colonies in the war of the Revolution that was to follow. Be that as it may, I do not hesitate to assert that whatever the course he would have taken, the majority of inhabitants of Tryon County would have followed him, in which case there would have been no Oriskany, no siege of Fort Schuyler, no Wyoming or Cherry Valley, no Indian raids or desolation of the valley, and possibly no Saratoga.

Sir John, however, being of a different character from his father and not having the same degree of moral power over the population of Tryon County, either Indians or whites, antagonized the yeomanry from the very beginning of his succession to the titles and estates of Sir William, with his arrogance and assumption of superiority on account of his British education, and looked down upon the humble friends of his father as being but little better than human chattels, and not worthy to associate with him, a knight and baronet of the realm of Great Britain.

Wm. L. Stone gives an account of the first clash in Tryon County between the Tories and patriots. Shortly after the news of the battle of Lexington had been received, a public meeting of the patriots was held at the house of John Veeder in Caughnawaga (Fonda). It was attended by about three hundred people, who assembled, unarmed, for the purpose of deliberation, and also to erect a liberty-pole—a most hateful object in that day in the eyes of the loyalists. Among the Whigs on that occasion were Sampson Sammons and his two sons Jacob and Frederick. Before they had accomplished the object for which they had met, the proceedings were interrupted by the arrival of Sir John Johnson accompanied by his two brothers-in-law, Colonels Guy Johnson and Daniel Claus, together with Col. John Butler and a large number of retainers armed with swords and pistols. Guy Johnson mounted a high stoop and harangued the people at length, and with great vehemence. He dwelt upon the strength and power of the King and was very virulent in his language toward the disaffected, causing their blood to boil with indignation. But they were unarmed and for the most part unprepared, if not indisposed, to proceed to any act of violence. The orator at length became so abusive that Jacob Sammons waxing warm and zealous called him a liar and a villain. Guy Johnson descending from his rostrum seized

Sir John Johnson

Sammons by the throat and called him a d—d villain in return.

A scuffle ensued, during which one of the intruders struck Sammons with a loaded whip, knocking him down. On recovering from the momentary stupor of the blow he found one of Johnson's servants sitting astride of his body. A well-directed blow relieved him of the incubus, and springing to his feet he threw off his coat and prepared for a fight. Two pistols were presented to his breast, but not discharged as Sammons was again knocked down by the clubs of the loyalists, and severely beaten. On recovering his feet once more, he perceived that his Whig friends had all decamped with the exception of a few of the Fondas, Veeders, and Vischers. The loyalists also drew off, and Jacob Sammons returned to his father's house bearing on his body the first scars of the Revolutionary contest in Tryon County.

Although the patriots of Tryon County were well convinced of Sir John's loyalty to the King and had strong reasons to fear hostile proceeding on the part of Sir John and his two hundred Highlanders, the Tryon County Committee of Safety, determining to probe his intentions at once and to the bottom, sent him the following letter:

TRYON COUNTY COMMITTEE CHAMBERS,
Oct. 26, 1775.

HONORABLE SIR:—
As we find particular reason to be convinced of your opinion in the questions hereafter expressed, we require you, that you'll please to oblige us with your sentiments thereupon in a few lines by our messengers, the bearers hereof, Messrs.

Ebenezer Cox, James McMaster, and John James Klock, members of our Committee.

We want to know whether you will allow that the inhabitants of Johnstown and Kingsborough may form themselves into companies, according to the regulations of our Continental Congress, for the defence of our Country's cause; and whether your honor would be ready himself to give his personal assistance to the same purpose.

Also whether you pretend a prerogative to our County court-house and gaol, and would hinder or interrupt the Committee, to make use of the same public houses, to our want and service in a common cause?

We don't doubt you will comply with our reasonable requests, and thereby oblige, Honorable Sir,
    Your most humble and obedient servants.
    By order of the Committee.
      NICHOLAS HERKIMER,
        Chairman.

To the Honorable SIR JOHN JOHNSON
 Johnson Hall.

To this letter Sir John replied—

That as to embodying his tenants, he never did or should forbid them; but they might save themselves further trouble, as he knew his tenants would not consent. Concerning himself, sooner than lift his hand against his King, or sign any association, he would suffer his head to be cut off. As to the gaol and Court-house, he would not deny the use of it for the purpose for which it was built, but that they were his property until he should be refunded seven hundred pounds. [He further said] he had been informed that two thirds of Canajoharie and German Flats people had been forced to sign the Association.

Although counselled by the Congress to refrain from any overt acts against the Johnsons, the people of Tryon County were much incensed against the

Sir John Johnson

Johnstown loyalists, particularly so when it became evident that Sir John was making preparations to fortify Johnson Hall and to garrison the same with his Highland retainers, and, as rumor declared, three hundred Iroquois savages, who were to sally out and ravage the surrounding country. I have called the Iroquois savages, but Mrs. Grant of Laggan, whom whom I have quoted before, pertinently asks:

> Were they savages, who had fixed habitations; who cultivated rich fields; who built castles (for so they called their not incommodious wooden houses surrounded with stockades); who planted maize and beans and showed great ingenuity in constructing and adorning their canoes, arms and clothing; they who had wise unwritten laws and conducted their wars, treaties, and alliances with deep and sound policy; they whose eloquence was bold and nervous and animated; whose language was sonorous, musical and expressive; who possessed generous and elevated sentiments, heroic fortitude and unstained probity?

In regard to the body of Roman Catholic Highlanders that Sir John had surrounded himself with, they were particularly obnoxious to the Protestant Palatines, not only on account of their swaggering arrogance and belted claymores, but because they detested their religion. The Johnsons and their friends, however, made no further efforts to meet their opponents, but stood strictly on the defensive, and the palisades, if ever completed, were not garrisoned by the Iroquois.

About this time Guy Johnson received warnings of a plot to kidnap him. He at once assembled the officers of his department and a party of trusty men of his own regiment of militia and fortified his house (known as Guy Park, on the Mohawk River about two miles east of Fort Johnson) to resist attack. A body of Mohawks gathered there to defend him and for the time being the mansion resembled a frontier fort. Colonel Guy was closely watched and attacks threatened, but no overt move was made on the part of the patriots.

It may be of interest to know that the first trace of actual activity on the part of Joseph Brant (Thayendanega) is a letter written by him at Guy Park, in the name of Aaron, John, and another Mohawk chief, in May, 1775, to the chiefs of the Oneidas urging them to come to the assistance of Colonel Guy Johnson. This letter was intercepted, and as the Oneidas failed to appear, Colonel Guy Johnson, accompanied by the officers of his department, a body-guard of Mohawks, and about a hundred Tories among whom were Daniel Claus, John and Walter Butler, Barent Frey, Han Yost Herkimer, Gilbert Tice, Joseph Brant, William and Peter, half-breed sons of Sir William Johnson, besides other men of weight and influence, marched rapidly up the valley and disappeared in the recesses of the Indian country. A majority of the party arrived in Montreal in August, 1775.

Sir John remained in the Mohawk Valley after Colonel Guy Johnson's departure, and, strong in his tenants and in his local influence, bid defiance to the Committee of Safety, and began to arm his tenants. His intention being suspected, General Philip Schuyler with four thousand troops marched to Johnstown, disarmed his tenants, and took him

Fireplace and Oven, Guy Park.

Sir John Johnson

prisoner. He was sent to Fishkill, where he was liberated on parole. The following May, however, Sir John, regardless of his promise, broke his parole and, accompanied by his Highlanders and other tenants, fled to Montreal by the way of Sacondaga and the Adirondack wilderness. Their route was probably through the lake region of Hamilton and Franklin counties to the St. Lawrence River at St. Regis. This seems to be proved from the fact that near the angle of junction of the St. Lawrence and Hamilton county line, and in the vicinity of Big Tupper Lake, a brass cannon and carriage lies nearly buried in the accumulation of the muck of the forest. It is said that a large forest tree has grown to a great height through one of the tires of a decayed wheel.

The exodus of Sir John and his followers was so hurried that they had no time to collect provisions, and during the nine days they were in the forests the whole party lived entirely upon wild onions, roots, and leaves of beech trees. Their feet became sore from travelling, and several of their number dropped out from exhaustion from time to time in the wilderness and were afterward brought in by Indians sent out for that purpose. During the nineteen days which elapsed between the time he left Johnstown and his arrival at Montreal, the party endured all the suffering that it seems possible for man to endure and live.

Of course Lady Johnson remained at the Hall, but was soon removed to Albany by Colonel Dayton, where she was retained as a kind of hostage for the peaceful conduct of her husband.

Upon Sir John's arrival in Montreal he was immediately commissioned a colonel in the British service, and raised a command of two battalions, composed of those who accompanied him in his flight, and other American loyalists and others who had followed their example. They were called the Royal Greens, probably from the color of their uniform. In the month of January, 1777, he found his way to New York city, then in the hands of the British forces.

It is probable that the loadstone that drew him there was his young wife, who subsequently escaped from her captivity. From that time he became one of the bitterest foes of his own contrymen of any who engaged in that contest.

CHAPTER VI

OGHWAGA IN THE SUSQUEHANNA VALLEY—MOHAWKS AT OGHWAGA AND ORISKANY—INTERVIEW BETWEEN GENERAL HERKIMER AND JOSEPH BRANT —MOLLIE BRANT DRIVEN FROM INDIAN CASTLE BY THE ONEIDAS

IN the eighteenth-century history of the Mohawk Valley and the Mohawks the name Oghwaga is frequently met, but in a vague, indefinite way, that leaves the reader in doubt of its locality or the particular tribe to which it belonged. Later investigation, however, brings to light the fact that it was located on the Susquehanna River near the confluence of the Unadilla River and the Cherry Valley Creek, which form the upper waters of the Susquehanna. It is thought to have existed as early as 1650, and was a primitive trading post for the Delaware, Susquehanna, and far western Indians, who there met the Dutch and English traders from Albany, and later Schenectady. Halsey quotes Stone as saying that the place was an aboriginal Port Royal, where many of the Six Nations who had become disgusted with the politics of their several cantons were in the habit of settling.

Whatever may have been its origin, it was evidently

a place of considerable importance as early as 1750, and under the jurisdiction of the Iroquois. It is said that many Mohawks and Oneidas dwelt there, and it was probably the third village or castle during the last French war, the others being the Canajorhees at Indian Castle, and the Mohawks proper at the old established village of Tiononderoga, at Fort Hunter. F. W. Halsey in *The Old New York Frontier* has given us the best account of that interesting locality that has been written. J. R. Simms speaks of a large tribe of Schoharie Indians. It is probable that he has confounded them with the Oghwagas.

W. L. Stone has transcribed, in his *Life of Brant*, a singular document, which I have never seen printed elsewhere, purporting to be a speech of Oneida warriors delivered to Colonel Elmore at Fort Schuyler, January 19, 1777:

BROTHER: We are sent here by the Oneida chiefs in conjunction with Onondagas. They arrived at our village yesterday. They gave us the melancholy news that the grand council-fire at Onondaga was extinguished. We have lost of their town by death ninety, among whom are three principal sachems. We, the remaining part of the Onondagas, do now inform our brethren that there is no longer a council-fire at the capital of the Six Nations. However, we are determined to use our feeble endeavors to support peace through the confederate nations. But let this be kept in mind, that the council-fire is extinguished. It is of importance that this be immediately communicated to General Schuyler, and likewise to our brothers the Mohawks. In order to effect this, we deposit this belt with Te-key-an-e-don-hot-te, Col. Elmore, commander at Fort Schuyler, who is sent here by General Schuyler to transact all matters relative to peace. We therefore request him to forward this intel-

In the Susquehanna Valley

ligence in the first place to Gen. Herkimer, desiring him to communicate it to the Mohawk castle near to him and then to Major Fonda, requesting him to immediately communicate it to the Lower Mohawk castle. Let the belt then be forwarded to General Schuyler, that he may know that our council-fire is extinguished and can no longer burn.

W. L. Stone remarks:

This singular document is worthy of preservation not only as the authentic but as the only account of the occurrence recorded. It contains a mystery, however, which cannot now be solved.

Undoubtedly the above speech was the occasion of great uneasiness throughout the Mohawk Valley, which was again awakened by the reported gathering of the Indians at Oghwaga. Scouts were moving along the borders, while a detachment of Continental troops kept at a distance small bodies of Indians and Tories. In February Colonel Harper was sent to Oghwaga by the Provincial Congress with a letter to the Indians gathered there, to ascertain their intentions. Colonel Harper, having given private orders to the captains of his regiment to hold themselves in readiness in case their services should be required, departed on his mission accompanied by one Indian and one white man. Arriving on February 27th, he was well received by the Indians and assured that the report of a contemplated invasion was untrue.

Satisfied with the sincerity of their professions he caused an ox to be roasted and invited the Indians to the barbecue, who at that time expressed their sorrow on account of the troubles of the country, and declared that they would take no part against it.

After returning from the mission the Colonel was, for a time, in command of one of the small Schoharie forts. In March or April of the same year he had occasion to go alone through the woods from Schoharie to his home at Harpersfield, and thence, when returning, struck to the westward toward the head waters of the Susquehanna. While ascending a hill he suddenly saw a company of Indians approaching. As they had discovered him, any attempt to fly would have been fatal. Having a great coat over his military dress, he made no attempt to avoid a meeting, and in passing the Colonel and the Indians exchanged salutations. One of the Indians he recognized as a Mohawk called Peter, whom he had formerly seen at Oghwaga.

They did not recognize him, however, but from his manner of speech supposed him to be a loyalist, and under that impression informed him that their intention was to cut off the "Johnstone settlement," a small Scotch colony on the eastern shore of the Susquehanna, near Unadilla. Quietly pursuing his way until out of sight of the hostile Indians he changed his course, hurried back to Harpersfield, collected a body of fifteen resolute men, and gave chase to the marauders. In addition to their arms and a requisite supply of food, he directed each man of his command to take with him a rope. In the course of the following night they discovered the camp-fire of the Indians on the bank of the Charlotte River. Halting for a while to rest and refresh themselves and prepare for the contest, the Colonel and his men advanced with great caution, prepared for an

Captain Joseph Brant.

instant dash upon the sleeping foe at the first sign of alarm. It was almost daylight and the Indians were in profound slumber, with their arms stacked in the middle of their encampment. Harper and his party silently removed the guns to a place of safety as a measure of precaution. When all was ready each man singled out his antagonist and advanced stealthily, with cords in readiness, until they stood over each sleeping foe, when, at a signal from Harper, they threw themselves upon the prostrate Indians and after a short and desperate struggle bound them securely. When daylight came Peter discovered his captor. "Huh!" he exclaimed, "Colonel Harper—why did not I know you yesterday?" The intrepid Colonel proceeded to Albany with his prisoners and surrendered them to the commanding officer of the station.

After the visit of Colonel Harper to Oghwaga in February, 1777, Thayendanega (Joseph Brant), having had some difficulty with Colonel Guy Johnson, came to Oghwaga with about ninety of his warriors, mostly Mohawks. The march of so large a body of warriors across the country added not a little uneasiness to the settlers, and to the Tryon County Committee of Safety. Although Brant, so far, had not committed any act of hostility within the province of New York, his presence did not improve the pacific intentions of the many Indians gathered on the banks of the Susquehanna, and in the end led to an open rupture. In June a large body of Indians, under Brant, ascended the Susquehanna from Oghwaga to Unadilla and requested an interview with

Rev. Mr. Johnstone and the militia officers at that place, and demanded food. Having required the people of that settlement to furnish his warriors with provisions, Brant told the officers that he had entered the British service and would not allow any of the Mohawks to be seized and confined to their castles, as he understood had been done. They remained two days at Unadilla, and when they left drove off some cattle and sheep. At this time the Mohawks at the lower castle (Fort Hunter), under Little Abraham, had not been drawn away by Brant and Guy Johnson, while at the upper castle (at Danube) Molly Brant remained with a number of Mohawks.

(Orders having been given somewhat later to destroy the habitation of the Mohawks at Fort Hunter and to drive them out of the valley, it was found that there were but four families left. These were ordered to leave, but owing to the entreaties of the white settlers their houses were not burned.)

Upon Brant's return to Oghwaga he received reinforcements and his attitude was so threatening that it was determined by General Schuyler that General Herkimer should confer with the Mohawk chief, with whom he had been on friendly terms when they had been neighbors beside the Mohawk River. Accordingly he sent a messenger inviting the Mohawk chief to meet him at Unadilla—the General moving forward himself at the same time at the head of about three hundred of the local militia. There Herkimer remained for eight days, or until the 27th of June, before Thayendanega arrived with five hundred warriors, who were established in camp about two miles

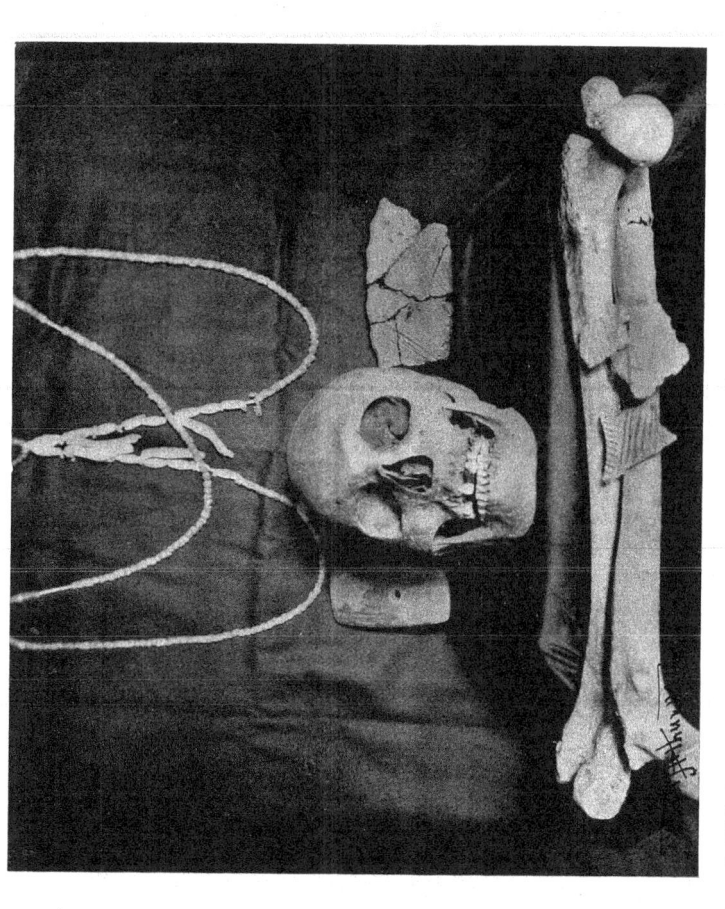

Skull and Thigh-bones and Broken Pottery Found in Mound Grave at Fort Hunter, N.Y. Also Copper Beads and Shell Ornament Found in Indian Grave near Coxsackie, N. Y.

General Herkimer and Joseph Brant 75

south of Unadilla. From this camp he despatched a runner to General Herkimer, with a message, desiring to be informed of the object of his visit. General Herkimer replied that he had merely come to see and converse with his brother, Captain Brant. The quick-witted messenger inquired if all those men wished to talk with the chief, too. But an arrangement was soon made by which a meeting was affected. The following particulars relating to the interview are told by J. R. Simms, he having obtained them from Joseph Wagner of Fort Plain: At the first meeting of General Herkimer and Brant, the latter was attended by three other chiefs, William Johnson (*alias* Teg-che-un-to, a son of Sir William, by his first Indian wife, Caroline), who was afterward killed by the half-breed Spencer at Oriskany; Pool, a smart-looking fellow with curly hair, supposed part Indian and part negro, and a short dark-skinned Indian, the four being surrounded by about twenty noble-looking warriors.

When in his presence, Brant haughtily asked General Herkimer the object of his visit, which was readily made known, but seeing so many attendants the chief suspected the interview was sought for another purpose. Said Brant to Herkimer: "I have five hundred warriors at my command, and can in an instant destroy you and your party; but we are old friends and neighbors and I will not do it." Colonel Cox, a smart officer (afterward killed at the battle of Oriskany), who accompanied General Herkimer, exchanged several sarcastic expressions with Brant, which served not a little to irritate him and his followers. The two had quarrelled a few years previous about lands around the upper Indian castle. Provoked to anger Brant asked Cox if he was not the son-in-law of "old George Klock." "Yes!" replied Cox, "what is that to you, you d—d Indian?" At the close of this dialogue Brant's guard ran off to their camp, firing several guns and making the forests ring with savage war cries. General Herkimer in the meantime endeavored to calm the storm which the impetuous Colonel had raised by his intemperate words, and succeeded in soothing the chief and his warriors and in keeping the irate Indians at a proper distance. A word from Brant hushed the tempest of passion, which an instant before threatened to deluge the valley in blood. However, as the parties were too heated for calm discussion, Brant said to the General: "It is needless to multiply words at this time; I will meet you here at nine o'clock to-morrow morning," and turning abruptly quickly joined his warriors.

It is presumed that General Herkimer, owing to the fierce looks of the turbulent warriors, feared treachery on the part of Brant at the coming interview, for early on the following morning he called Joseph Wagner, then an active young soldier, to his side and asked him if he could keep a secret. When assured in the affirmative, he instructed Wagner to select three trusty comrades, who with himself should be in readiness at a given signal to shoot Brant and the three chiefs, if the interview about to take place did not end amicably.

With this arrangement of precaution on the part

Junction of the Mohawk and Schoharie Rivers with Erie Canal Aqueduct.

General Herkimer and Joseph Brant 77

of General Herkimer, the parties held their interview on the 28th of June. Brant was the first to speak. Said he: "General Herkimer, I now fully comprehend the object of your visit, but you are too late; I am already engaged to serve the King. We are old friends and I can do no less than let you return home unmolested, although you are entirely within my power, as I have five hundred warriors with me armed and ready for battle." Saying which, at a signal a host of his armed warriors darted forth from the contiguous forest all painted and ready for battle as the well-known war-whoop but too clearly proclaimed. He then requested that the Rev. Mr. Stuart, the missionary of Queen Anne's Chapel at Fort Hunter, and the wife of Colonel Butler, living at the same place, be permitted to retire to Canada. To these requests the General assented, and, after presenting Brant ten or twelve heads of cattle, he struck camp and retraced his steps to the valley of the Mohawk, while Brant turned proudly away and disappeared in the depths of the forest, little knowing by what a slender thread hung his life as he gave the signal for the spectacular display of his painted warriors.

W. L. Stone says:

Thus terminated this most singular conference. It was early in July, and the morning was remarkably clear and beautiful. But the echo of the war-whoop had scarcely died away before the heavens became black, and a violent storm obliged each party to seek the nearest shelter. Men less superstitious than many of the unlettered yeomen who, leaning upon their arms, were witnesses of the events of this day could not fail in after times to look back upon the tempest, if not as an omen, at least as an emblem of those bloody massacres with which these Indians and their associates afterward visited the inhabitants of this unfortunate frontier.

This was the last conference held with the hostile Mohawks. Previous to this time a feeling of uncertainty and great unrest, as to the course of the Mohawks, pervaded the valley. A few families of Indians still remained at Fort Hunter and at the upper castle—at Danube,—who professed neutrality. At Fort Hunter dwelt Little Abraham, while at Indian Castle Molly Brant was living at the home of her brother.

After the conference between General Herkimer and Joseph Brant recorded above, Brant left the Mohawk Valley and proceeded to Oswego with his warriors, having been summoned to attend a general grand council of the Six Nations. At this assembly the chiefs were offered ample reward to enter the British service, but many of them were averse to joining in the war, as they considered themselves bound to neutrality by the recent treaty of German Flats and Albany. A protracted discussion ensued, which availed nothing to the commissioners until they appealed to the avarice of the Indians, saying: "The King is rich and powerful, both in money and subjects. His rum is as plentiful as the waters of Lake Ontario and his men as numerous as the sands upon its shore, and if you will assist the British in the war you will never want for goods or money." Overcome by a rich display of tawdry articles calculated to please their fancies the Indians proved recreant to their treaty with Gen-

General Herkimer and Joseph Brant 79

eral Schuyler and concluded an alliance with Great Britain, binding themselves to take up the hatchet against the rebels until they were subdued.

At the close of the treaty, each Indian was given a suit of clothes, a brass kettle, a gun, a tomahawk and scalping knife, a quantity of ammunition, a piece of gold, and the promise of a bounty for every scalp they should bring in (eight dollars for adults and a smaller sum for children). From that day Thayendanega was the acknowledged head of the Six Nations, and joining Colonel Bird at Oswego, with his command, proceeded to the investment of Fort Schuyler, which led to the subsequent siege and the attendant bloody ambuscade of Oriskany.

At this time from her temporary home at Canajoharie, or Indian Castle, Molly Brant sent a message to Brant by an Indian runner warning him that a body of nearly a thousand militia under Herkimer was on the march to relieve the garrison of said fort.

There can be no doubt but what his sister Molly kept him posted in regard to affairs in the valley and furnished him much valuable information previous to her forcible removal from thence.

During the siege of Fort Schuyler, the Indians with St. Leger took occasion to chastise the Oneidas, who had refused to unite with them. After the battle of Oriskany, Brant and a party of his warriors fell upon the old Oneida castle, burned the wigwams, destroyed the crops and drove away the cattle of his former confederates. No sooner had he retreated, however, than the Oneidas retaliated. The residence of Molly Brant, at the upper Mohawk castle (Danube), was ravaged, herself and family driven from home, and her cash, clothing and cattle taken. From thence the avengers visited the lower castle, and drove the followers of Little Abraham, one hundred in number, to refuge in Montreal, laying waste their plantations. Molly fled to Onondaga, and besought vengeance for the indignities which she had suffered, but to her possessions she was never restored: the indignant Oneidas had blotted out forever the seats of power from whence her tribe had swayed the destinies of a once powerful people.

Auburey—Batten Kill, N. Y.: "The Mohawk Nation," says Auburey, "which are called Sir William Johnson's Indians, as having their villages near his plantations, and who in his life time was constantly among them, were driven from their villages by the Americans and have joined our army [British]. They have come with their squaws, children, cattle, horses, and sheep, and are encamped at the creek from whence this place takes its name [Batten Kill].

"When the army cross the river, the squaws and children are to go to Canada. Brant and his warriors are said to have been with them." Like the other Indians, the Mohawks soon became impatient under the restriction imposed upon their movements by the presence of so large an army, and they deserted Burgoyne some time before the catastrophe of Saratoga. Molly Brant was probably with them also.

A Corner of Old St. George's Churchyard, Schenectady, N. Y.

CHAPTER VII

RÉSUMÉ OF HISTORY OF THE WAR IN THE VALLEY—
THE GLEN-SANDERS HOUSE—OLD DOCUMENTS—
THE DIARY OF WILLIAM COLBRAITH—THE KILLING
OF THE MAIDENS—THE FIRST RAISING OF THE
STARS AND STRIPES OVER AN AMERICAN FORT—
COLONEL WILLETT'S SORTIE—THE DEFEAT OF ST.
LEGER

IN a former volume, *The Mohawk Valley, Its Legends and Its History* considerable prominence is given to the battle of Oriskany and the siege of Fort Schuyler, together with the sortie of Colonel Willett, which resulted in the destruction of the camps of the Indians and the dispersion of Sir John Johnson's body-guards. Herewith will be found a diary of William Colbraith, a soldier of the garrison, which sheds additional light on the siege and interesting information not hitherto published.

At the beginning of the Revolution Montgomery County (called Tryon County from 1772 to 1784) was without limit, reaching westward through the wilderness as far as the territory of New York province extended.

The Mohawk Valley, the home of the Agniers or Mohawks, early became the route of Indian traders to Lake Ontario and the wilderness of the great West, as the Mohawk River was navigable to the birchen canoes of the Indians and the bateaux of the white men. In 1758 a stockade fort was built at Utica and named Fort Schuyler, for Col. Peter Schuyler. It is said to have stood between Mohawk and Main streets below Second Street. There was no settlement at Utica at that time; in fact, it is said that there were but three log huts at this place in 1787. The fort at Utica was allowed to decay after the French war, and was not in existence in 1777.

The city of Rome, at the head of the boat navigation, early became an important point with the Indian traders or merchants, and was known as the carrying place from the Mohawk River to Wood Creek, a mile away. Goods were transferred from the Mohawk River to Wood Creek, down which boats were poled or paddled to Oneida Lake, through the lake to Oswego River, and thence to Lake Ontario.

In 1725 a fort was built midway between the Mohawk and Wood Creek and named Fort Bull, and on the Mohawk, east of the present site of Rome, Fort Williams was erected. Fort Bull was destroyed March 27, 1756, by a party of French and Indians under M. DeLery, and the same year Fort Williams was destroyed by General Webb, he deeming it untenable. During the Revolution a fortification called Fort Newport was erected on Wood Creek near the carrying place.

Fort Stanwix, at Rome, N. Y., received its name from Brigadier-General John Stanwix, who began the construction of this fort July 23, 1758. It was located near the south bank of the river, about thirty rods

Résumé of War in the Valley 83

distant. It is said to have been a square work of earth and timber with bastions at each corner, surrounded by a ditch and mounted with heavy cannon.

This fort was also allowed to decay, so that when Colonel Dayton took possession of it in 1776 it is said to have been untenable. Colonel Dayton was charged with repairing Fort Stanwix, and renamed it Fort Schuyler, for General Philip Schuyler. He did not, however, make much headway in putting it in a defensible condition, as we learn that Colonel Gansevoort when he took command of the fort, in the spring of 1777, was obliged to use strenuous measures to strengthen its defences. However, it proved to be equal to the emergency of resisting the attack of St. Leger, as that general says, in his report of the subsequent siege: "It was found that our cannon had not the least effect on the sodwork of the fort, and that our royals had only the power of teasing, as a six-inch plank was a sufficient security for their powder magazine, as we learned from the deserters."

The story of the siege of Fort Schuyler has been so often told that I will not, at this time, do any more than outline the situation of military affairs in this part of the State in the early years of the Revolution. In 1777 "Burgoyne's plan" had been inaugurated and the campaign was in full swing. This plan, you will remember, was arranged in London and comprised an advance of troops under General Howe up the Hudson, Burgoyne's advance up the Champlain Valley and down the upper Hudson, while St. Leger was to proceed from Three Rivers in Canada to Oswego with a body of English and Canadian troops under Sir John

Johnson and Colonel John Butler and a horde of Canadian Indians under Joseph Brant, the whole force being under command of Colonel Barry St. Leger. It was planned that St. Leger should proceed from Oswego to Rome, destroy or capture Fort Schuyler, and then march through the Mohawk Valley, carrying death and destruction in his train, while Burgoyne and Howe should clear the valleys of Champlain and Hudson, the rendezvous of all three expeditions to be Albany, which they were all expected to reach simultaneously. How General Howe failed to ascend the Hudson, how Burgoyne's advance was checked at Bennington and his army captured at Saratoga, is well known to history; but early records of this campaign do not seem to recognize the importance of the battle of Oriskany, in clearing Tryon County and the balance of New York State, west of the Hudson River, of the British troops. Many of the old accounts of the battle characterize it as an ignominious defeat, ending with a cowardly retreat of the Americans, when it was, in fact, one of the most heroic, stubborn and decisive battles of the Revolution. It is true that General Herkimer was defeated in his attempt to march his troops to Fort Schuyler and to assist Colonel Gansevoort in the siege of the fort, but he fought his troops coolly and courageously under the most disadvantageous circumstances, and finally compelled the British and their hired allies, the Indians, to retreat and leave the battle-field to the nearly exterminated band of patriots and their fatally wounded general.

It will be remembered that before General Herkimer

Glen-Sanders House, Scotia, N. Y., 1713.

Résumé of War in the Valley

advanced from Fort Dayton (Herkimer) he sent Adam Helmer and two other trusty men through the wilderness, and at the risk of their lives, to inform Colonel Gansevoort of his advance with eight hundred soldiers, and requesting the commandant to give three cannon shots when the three scouts should arrive at the fort; and also requested Colonel Gansevoort to make a sortie of troops in order to divert the attention of the besiegers from the advance of General Herkimer and his eager and impetuous but undisciplined soldiers.

I have deemed it best to write this summary of the situation of affairs in the Mohawk Valley during August, 1777, in order to place before you some new material in regard to the siege of the fort.

On the north bank of the Mohawk River, opposite the city of Schenectady, is the little village of Scotia; so named by one of the first settlers in the vicinity of Schenectady, who was called, by his Dutch neighbors, Sanders Leendertse Glen, but whose Scotch name was Alexander Lindsey Glen. He came to this country by the way of Holland in 1633 and some years later (about 1658) settled on land at Scotia.

A few rods west of the toll bridge that spans the Mohawk at Schenectady stands the old Glen-Sanders house, so called in later years on account of the intermarriage of the two families. It is said that a sister of Alexander Glen married a man by the name of Sanders, and that the present owners of the old house, husband and wife, are both lineal descendants from the father of Alex. Leendertse Glen, the families again being brought together after nearly three centuries. It is said that a house was erected on the north bank of the Mohawk near the site of the present building by Glen, the first settler, about 1660. A half-century later, or, to be more exact, in 1713, the river having encroached upon the old structure to such an extent as to render it unsafe for occupancy, a new dwelling was erected on higher ground, much of the older building being used in its construction, which can be seen at the present day, in many of the doors and casings. The family, proud of their ancestors and the antiquity of their surroundings, have preserved their home and its antique furniture, together with old letters and legal documents, so that to-day it is a storehouse of treasures of historic value; its large collection of old china and quaint furniture making it a most interesting museum to antiquaries of the historic Mohawk Valley. The writer, at a recent visit, was shown no less than five parchment commissions, to members of the Glen family, alternately bearing the signatures of the colonial governors, Lords Bellamont, Sloughter, Fletcher, Dongan, and Hunter, and one signed by Morris. Many of the documents which have been preserved have lain *perdu* in old chests without examination for many years.

One of these chests has recently undergone inspection, which has brought to light the commissions spoken of above, together with a very interesting paper which proves to be a diary of a soldier of Colonel Gansevoort's regiment, having been kept by a member of the detachment of Major Cochran, sent to reinforce Colonel Elmore at Fort Schuyler April 17,

Glen–Sanders House

1777, and bears a striking resemblance to Colonel Willett's report to Governor Trumbull after the termination of the siege, with many interesting particulars of life within the fort not mentioned by Willett in his report. It covers the period between April 17, 1777, when Colonel Gansevoort's troops relieved Colonel Elmore, and August 23d of the same year, the day General Benedict Arnold entered the fort after the hurried retreat of St. Leger's troops.

It also gives the date (August 3, 1777) when the first American flag, of the regulation Stars and Stripes, was raised above an American fort, having been made by the inhabitants of the fort from a blue cloak, a red flannel skirt, and strips of white cotton.

The manuscript begins as follows:

1777—Journal of the most material occurrences preceding the siege of Fort Schuyler (formerly Fort Stanwix) with an account of that siege, etc.

April 17th.—A detachment of Colonel Gansevoort's regiment, under command of Major Cochran, arrived to reinforce Colonel Elmore, who was stationed there.

May 3d.—Colonel Gansevoort arrived and took command of the garrison agreeable to instructions.

May 10th.—Colonel Elmore's regiment march for Albany.

May 28th.—The remainder of the regiment under the command of Colonel Willett arrived here from Fort Constitution, who informed Colonel Gansevoort that by order of Major Gen. Gates he had relieved Fort Dayton, (then in charge of Lieutenant Colonel Livingston), with one captain, two subalterns, two sergeants, one drum and fife and forty rank and file of his detachment. Some Oneida Indians arrived here with a flag from Canada, who informed the Colonel that they had been to Caughnawaga to request them not to take up the hatchet in favor of Great Britain and gave him assurance of that tribe being much inclined to keep the peace, that had for so long a time subsisted between them and their American brethren, and that some of the sachems would be here in eight days on their way for Albany to treat on this subject. And also, as they were going to Canada they met the enemy on their march from thence to Oswego, being destined for this place, and after the treaty was over, which Sir John Johnson was to hold with the Indians in that country at Oswego, we might hourly expect them.

June 25th.—Capt. Grigg, with Corporal Maddeson of his company, being between the Forts Newport and Bull, about $1\frac{1}{4}$ miles from Fort Schuyler, were attacked by a party of Indians who wounded and tomahawked them and scalped them. The captain was alive when found, but the corporal dead.

July 3d.—Ensign Sporr, being in command of seven men cutting sods for the fort at Fort Newport, were attacked by a party of Indians, who killed and scalped one, wounded and scalped another, and took the ensign and four men prisoners.

July 19th.—Capt. Grigg, being much recovered of his wounds, set off for Albany.

July 19th.—Same day arrived Captain Swartwout, Lieutenants Diefendorf, Ball, Welch, McClellan, Bowen, Ostrander and Colbreath and Ensign Denniston, with a number of recruits for the regiment.

July 26th.—The sachems of Caughnawaga arrived here with a flag agreeable to the intelligence received from the Oneida Indians. A party of one hundred of the garrison went to guard a number of the militia sent to obstruct Wood creek by falling trees from either side into the creek.

July 27th.—Three girls belonging to the inhabitants being about two hundred yards from our out-sentinels were fired on by a party of Indians, two of whom were killed and scalped, the other wounded in two places, neither of them dangerous. The party returned who had been to stop the creek.

July 28th.—The Colonel sent off those women which belonged to the garrison which have children, with whom went

Col. Barry St. Leger.
From an old print.

the man that was scalped, the girl that was wounded yesterday and sick in the hospital.

July 30th.—An Indian arrived express from the Oneida castle with a belt of wampum and a letter from the sachems of Caughnawaga and the Six Nations, in which letter they assured us they were determined to be at peace with the American brethren; that the enemy were at the Three Rivers and two detachments were to set off before the main body; one body of eight would be sent to take prisoners, and another of 130 to cut off communication on the Mohawk river. Major Bedlam arrived with 150 men of Colonel Weston's regiment from Fort Dayton; with him came Captain Dewitt and his party who had been left at Fort Dayton by Colonel Willett, the whole making to the garrison a reinforcement of about 200 men. Mr. Hansen, commissary of this garrison, arrived and acquainted us that seven bateaux, loaded with ammunition and provisions, were on their way for this place. The letter and belt was, agreeable to the request of the Indians, sent down by express to the several committees on the Mohawk river.

Aug. 1st.—Three Oneida Indians came express from their castle informing us that they had seen three strange Indians, who told them that there were 100 more at the Royal Block House, and that they were to march for this place. Supposing them to be a party sent to cut off communications, the Colonel detached 100 men under command of Captain Benschoten and three subalterns to meet the bateaux that were hourly expected, in order to reinforce the guard sent with them from Fort Dayton.

Aug. 2d.—Four bateaux arrived, being those the party went to meet, having a guard of 100 men of Colonel Weston's regiment from Fort Dayton, under the command of Lieut. Col. Mellon of that regiment. The lading being brought safe into the fort, guard marched in, when our sentinels on the southwest bastion discovered the enemy's fires in the woods near Fort Newport, upon which the troops ran to their respective alarm posts; at this time we discovered some men running from the landing toward the garrison. On their coming they informed us that the bateaux men who had staid behind when the guard marched into the fort had been fired on by the enemy at the landing, that two of them were wounded, the master of the bateaux taken prisoner, and one man missing.

Aug. 3d.—Early this morning a Continental flag, made by the officers of Colonel Gansevoort's regiment, was hoisted and a cannon leveled at the enemy's camp was fired on the occasion. A small party was sent to the landing to see if the enemy had destroyed any of our bateaux last night. This party found the bateaux man that was missing, wounded through the brain, stabbed in the right breast and scalped. He was alive when found and brought to the garrison, but died shortly after. The bateaux lay at the landing no ways damaged. About 3 o'clock this afternoon the enemy showed themselves to the garrison on all sides, carried off some hay from a field near the garrison, at which a flag brought by Captain Tice came into the fort with a proffer of protection if the garrison would surrender, which was rejected with disdain.

Aug. 4th.—A continual firing of small arms was this day kept up by the enemy's Indians, who advanced within gunshot of the fort, in small parties under cover of bushes, weeds and potatoes in the garden. Colonel Mellon and his party of 100 men, who came from Fort Dayton as a guard to the bateaux, was to have returned this day, but we were now besieged and all communication cut off for the present. The firing ended with the close of the day, we having one man killed and six wounded. This night we sent out a party and brought 27 stacks of hay into the trench and set a barn and house on fire belonging to Mr. Roof.

Aug. 5th.—A continual firing was kept up by the savages. One of our men was shot dead on the northeast bastion. The enemy set fire to the new barracks standing about 100 yards from this fort, between four and five o'clock this afternoon.

Aug. 6th.—This morning the Indians were seen going off from around the garrison towards the landing; as they withdrew we had not much firing. Being uneasy lest the Tories should report that the enemy had taken the fort, Lieut. Diefendorf was ordered to get ready to set off for Albany this evening to inform General Schuyler of our situation, but between nine and ten this morning three militia men arrived here with a letter from General Harkeman wherein he writes that he had arrived at Orisco with 1,000 militia, in order to relieve the garrison and open communication, which was then entirely blocked up, and that if the colonel should hear a firing of small arms, desired he would send a party from the garrison to reinforce him. General Harkeman desired that the colonel would fire three cannon, if the three men got safe into the fort with his letter, which was done and followed by three cheers by the whole garrison. According to General Harkeman's request the colonel detached two hundred men and one field piece under command of Lieut. Col. Willett with orders to proceed down the road to meet the General's party; having marched half a mile, they came upon an encampment of the enemy which they totally routed, and plundered them of as much baggage as the soldiers could carry. Their loss is supposed to be between fifteen and twenty killed. The number of wounded, who got off, is unknown. They took four prisoners, three of whom were wounded, and Mr. Singleton of Montreal, who says he is a lieutenant, without the loss of one man killed or wounded. Our party returned immediately and brought in a number of blankets, brass kettles, powder and ball, a variety of clothes and Indian trinkets and hard cash, together with four scalps the Indians had lately taken, being entirely fresh and left in their camp. *Two of the scalps taken are supposed to be those of the girls, being neatly dressed and the hair plaited.* A bundle of letters was found in the enemy's camp, which had been sent by one Luke Cassidy for this garrison, who it is supposed is either killed or taken; the letters were not broke open. Four colours were also taken, and immediately hoisted on our flagstaff under the Continental flag, as trophies of victory. By our prisoners we learn that the enemy are 1210 strong, 250 British regulars, that they are all arrived and have with them two six pounders, two three pounders and four royals. We also learn that they were attacked by our militia on this side of Orisco, that they drove the militia back, killed some and took several prisoners, but the enemy had many killed, and among them one Stephen Watts of New York. Our party found among the enemy a Tory named Harkeman, brother to the General. He belonged to the German Flats. One of General Harkeman's militia came in here this evening and gave an account of the militia being drove back by the enemy, that in the battle he hid himself in the mud and grass, and that General Harkeman and a number of regular officers and Indians passed him in conversation. (This was a lie.) One of the prisoners we took to-day died of his wounds this evening.

Aug. 7th.—Very little firing to-day. At 11 o'clock this evening the enemy came near the fort, called to our sentinels, telling them to come out again with fixed bayonets, and they would give us satisfaction for yesterday's work; after which they fired four small cannon at the fort. We laughed at them and they returned to rest. The four militia men who came in yesterday went off about 12 o'clock this night. Two men deserted from us to the enemy this night.

Aug. 8th.—The enemy threw some shells at us to-day, but did no damage, and in order to return the compliment, they were saluted with a few balls from our cannon. About 5 o'clock this evening Colonel Butler, with a British captain and a doctor from the enemy, came to the garrison with a flag, whose message from Gen. St. Leger was that the Indians, having lost some of their chiefs in a skirmish with our party that sallied out on the 6th inst., were determined to go down the Mohawk River and destroy the women and children, also that they would kill every man in the garrison when they got in; that Gen. St. Leger had held a council with them for two days in order to prevent them, but all to no purpose,

Upper Onega Creek.

Colbraith's Journal

unless we would surrender. The general therefore, as an act of humanity, and to prevent the effusion of blood, begged we would deliver up the fort, and promised if we did, not a hair of our heads should be hurt. A letter also came by them (as they say) from Mr. Fry and Colonel Bellinger, whom they took in the fray with the militia, begging us to surrender, telling us our communication was cut off, that the enemy had a large parcel of fine troops, and an excellent park of artillery, and further, that they expected General Burgoyne was in Albany, and could see no hopes of our having any succor, as the militia had many killed and taken. The answer to the general's tender and compassioned (?) letter was deferred until to-morrow morning at 9 o'clock, and a cessation of arms agreed to by both parties till then. Late this evening a party was sent to get water for the garrison, with a guard. One of the guards deserted from us, but left his firelock behind. One of our sentinels fired at him but missed him. Our guard heard the enemy's sentinels challenge him twice and fire on him. Colonel Willett and Lieutenant Stockwell went out of the garrison at one o'clock in the morning on a secret expedition.

Aug. 9th.—Agreeable to the proposals of yesterday, between Colonel Gansevoort and Brigadier General St. Leger, a flag was sent out to him requesting him to send his demand in writing and the Colonel would send him an answer, which request he agreed to. The demands in writing was the same in substance with that verbally delivered yesterday by Colonel Butler, to which the Colonel returned for answer: That he was determined to defend the fort in favor of the United States to the last extremity. Upon receiving the answer hostilities again commenced by a number of shot and small arms on their side which were not suffered with impunity on ours. This day the Colonel ordered all the provisions to be brought upon the parade for fear of shells setting fire to the barracks and destroying it; also all the public papers and money in the hands of Mr. Hansen and the papers in the hands of Mr. Van Veghten belonging to the paymaster to be lodged in the bomb-proof in the S. W. bastion. The enemy began to bombard us at half past ten this evening and continued till daylight; their shells were very well directed. They killed one man and wounded another, both of our regiment. None killed or wounded through the day. This day the enemy kept out of sight, except one or two who appeared about their battery doing nothing. About three o'clock this afternoon three or four of them were seen running across a field near the garrison and setting fire to some cocks of hay standing there which soon consumed them. This manœuver of the enemy led us to believe that the enemy's intention was to deceive us to imagine thereby that they were going off and put us off our guard and induce us to send out parties which they might fall on, and thereby diminish our strength, knowing us to be too many for them. Was this their scheme, they fell short of their conjecture. Some of our officers imagined they were going off or they would not destroy the hay, it being out of our reach and much wanted by them for their troops to lay on, as it is certain they have nothing to shelter themselves from the weather except their blankets which they make tents of.

Fearing they meant to lull us to sleep and storm us in the night, the Colonel ordered the guard and piquet doubled and the troops to lay on their arms. Between twelve and one o'clock to-night they bombard us and continued till daylight. This night's work did us no other damage than breaking the thigh of a young man, an inhabitant. This unfortunate young man was brought up in the same family with one of the girls that was killed and scalped on the 27th, and whose scalps we have now in the fort. They were remarkably industrious and faithful, both orphans and were by consent of their former master to have been married very soon. The young man died of his wound.

Aug. 11th.—This day the enemy having observed that we brought water from the creek altered its course so that it became dry. This would have done us much damage had we not been able to open two wells in the garrison which with one we had already proved a sufficient supply. The enemy kept out of sight and no firing from them of any kind. They were seen by our sentinels drawing near the landing, by which we imagine a reinforcement is coming to our relief. At twelve o'clock a shower of rain coming up the Colonel ordered a fatigue party to turn out with a subaltern's guard to bring in some barrels of lime, a number of boards and some timber lying at the foot of the glacis. Which they effected without having a shot fired at them. The enemy was seen to muster in the road below the landing while our men were out. At sundown they gave us some shot and shells from their battery. At midnight they sent four shells, but a thunder shower coming up at that instant they left off. The night being very dark and excessive raining till day, the Colonel ordered the troops to their alarm posts lest the enemy should attempt to surprise.

Aug. 12th.—The enemy kept out of sight all day and no firing from them till noon, when they gave us some shot and shells, without doing any damage. We imagined the enemy drew their forces in the daytime between us and Orisko, as we have not seen them so plenty these two or three days as we are used to do; neither do they trouble us all night, which gave our troops an opportunity of resting.

Aug. 13th.—The enemy were very peaceable all day till towards night, when they cannonaded and bombarded for two hours, during which time a shell broke a soldier's leg belonging to Colonel Mellon's detachment.

Aug. 14th.—Toward evening they were again at their old play, cannonading and bombarding us. A shell bursting slightly wounded one of Colonel Mellon's men in the head. No other damage was done. One of Captain Gregg's company, Colonel Gansevoort's regiment, deserted his post to the enemy. He was placed on the outside picket and deserted between ten and twelve o'clock at night.

Aug. 15th.—At 5 o'clock this morning the enemy threw two shells at us. Did no damage. The number of shells they have thrown at us is 137. The enemy were very troublesome with their small arms this afternoon, by which we had one man of our regiment and one of Colonel Mellon's detachment slightly wounded. In the evening they threw their shells at us and slightly wounded a woman and one of Captain Savage's artillery-men.

Aug. 16th.—This morning the enemy threw some shells horizontally at our works, but fell short. One of those shells falling on the parade killed a man of Colonel Mellon's detachment. They continued to throw them all day and some part of the night, but did no further damage. A party of our men were ordered out this evening to bring in wood for the garrison, and being discovered by some skulking Indians near the garrison gave the alarm to the rest. They advanced near where our men were at work, but luckily our men had been called in before they came nigh enough to do any mischief. They finding our men had got in began a most hideous shout. A cannon being fired at them they departed. The regulars' drums were heard beating to arms after the cannon was fired. We suppose they expected us to sally out again upon them with a field-piece. At midnight they threw three shells at us, but did no damage.

Aug. 17th.—The enemy were quiet all day and night; neither a shot or shell was fired at us during the twenty-four hours, although we fired several cannon at them.

Aug. 18th.—This morning one of our regiment was slightly wounded in the cheek by a musquet ball. A black flag or coat was seen in enemy's bomb battery.

Aug. 19th.—The enemy threw some shells at us near noon. They were busy in their trench all day. At night they struck their trench towards the point of our northwest bastion, and by daylight had got within 150 yards of the ditch. We fired some grape shot at them now and then all night. At every shot we fired they threw shells at us but did no damage. At midnight the colonel sent out one of his regiment and one of Colonel Mellon's detachment to meet Colonel Willett if possible, whom we expected was on his way to this place with a reinforcement, to make him acquainted with the

Colbraith's Journal

enemy's maneuvers on the southwest side of the fort, that he might govern the attack accordingly.

Aug. 20th.—This morning one of Colonel Mellon's men was wounded by a musquet ball. The enemy could work but little this day at their trench, it being so nigh that our small arms, as well as our cannon shot, was too hot for them. In the evening they began their trench again and worked all night at it, under fire of our cannon and small arms, but did not approach any nearer.

Aug. 21st.—At two o'clock this morning a party was sent out to bring in firewood, who brought in a great quantity undiscovered. They cannonaded and bombarded by turns all night. A man of our regiment deserted this evening. This morning we discovered that the enemy approach nearer to us and had begun a bomb battery, where they left off yesterday morning. The artillery-man who was wounded in the knee with a musquet ball died on the 4th inst. of his wounds. One of Colonel Mellon's men and the lad belonging to the inhabitants died likewise of their wounds. The enemy kept working all day in their trench though not so close as last night. No firing from their batteries. This day our guard kept a constant fire at those at work in the trench, and in the evening twelve of the best marksmen were picked out to harass them when at work in the night, which galled them so much that their Indians were sent for to draw off our attention, who advanced near the fort, which caused a general alarm, by which a heavy and continued firing was kept up for near two hours, during which their cannon and mortars were playing on us very briskly, in which interim we had a man of the artillery wounded and a woman big with child wounded in the thigh. A corporal and three privates deserted this evening of our regiment.

Aug. 22d.—This morning the enemy bombarded very smartly. The sergeant-major and two privates were wounded. At noon a deserter came to us, whose examination was: that the enemy had news in the camp that Burgoyne's army was entirely routed and that three thousand men were coming up to reinforce us, and further that the enemy was retreating with great precipitation, and that he with another was conveying off one Lieut. Anderson's chest, when he had made his escape, and that most of the baggage was gone. Upon which the commanding officer ordered all the cannon bearing on their works to fire several rounds each to see whether they would return it, which partly confirmed the report of the deserter. Some time after four men came in and reported the same, and that they had left part of their baggage. Upon which the colonel ordered fifty men and two wagons under command of Captain Jansen to go to their camps, where they killed two Indians and took four prisoners; one of them was an Indian. After they had loaded the wagons with what baggage they could carry, they returned, but night coming on, they could not return to fetch what baggage was still left in their camp. At night, two men came in: one of them was assisting the first deserter in carrying off Lieutenant Anderson's chest, the other John (Han) Yost Schuyler, who informed the commanding officer that he was taken prisoner at the German Flats and confined at Fort Dayton five days. That General Arnold had sent him to General St. Leger, commander of the King's troop, to inform him that 2,000 Continentals with two field-pieces and a great number of militia were on the march for this place to reinforce the garrison, that he had informed General St. Leger of it and in consequence of which he ordered his troops to strike their tents and pack up. And further, after he had done his errand, he hid himself in the woods till night, and coming across the above men they came in together. He likewise informed us that near seventeen Indians were at Fort Newport quite drunk; upon which the colonel ordered a party of men under the command of Major Cochran to go and take them, who in about an hour returned and informed the colonel he had been there and did not find any, and that he went to Wood creek and found eight new bateaux, which the enemy had left behind. While they were out, the woman that was wounded with a shell last night was brought to bed in our

Old Mile Square Road, Onega Creek.

southwest bomb-proof, of a daughter. She and the child are like to do well, with the blessing of God. Our blockade ended, and the garrison once more at liberty to walk about and take the free air we had for twenty-one days been deprived of. At twelve o'clock this night the commanding officer sent off three of his regiment to inform General Arnold of the precipitate retreat of the enemy. A deserter came in who said he had just left the enemy's cohorns below Wood creek bridge.

Aug. 23d.—This morning the colonel sent out a party under the command of Major Cochran to take them, who returned with three prisoners and four cohorns and some baggage, and reported there were seventeen bateaux lying there. Another party was sent to the enemy's north camp to bring in the rest of the baggage left by us last night, consisting of ammunition, camp equipage and entrenching tools. Another party was sent to the enemy's southeast camp, who brought in fifteen wagons, a three-pound field-piece carriage with all its apparatus. Most of the wagon wheels were cut to pieces, as were the wheels of the carriage. Several scouts were sent out to-day, one of whom took a German prisoner, who reported that the enemy's Indians had, when they got about ten miles from this fort, fallen on the scattering Tories, took their arms from, and stabbed them with their own bayonets. And that for fear of said Indians, he and nine more German soldiers had took to the woods. The rest are not yet found. Their design was not to come to the fort, as Butler and Johnson told them, when orders were given to retreat, that those who fell into our hand would be hanged immediately. Another scout proceeded to Canada creek, found a carriage for a six-pounder and three boxes of cannon shot, which they brought in. This afternoon the Honorable Major General Arnold arrived here with near a thousand men. They were saluted with a discharge of powder from our mortars, formerly the enemy's, and all the cannon from the bastions, amounting in the whole to thirteen, attended with three cheers from the troops on the bastions.

CHAPTER VIII

CAPTURE OF WALTER BUTLER, HAN YOST SCHUYLER, AND OTHER TORIES—HAN YOST'S MISSION TO ST. LEGER'S ARMY—FLIGHT OF THE INDIANS—TERROR OF THE TORIES—RETREAT OF ST. LEGER

WHILE the army of St. Leger was investing Fort Schuyler, successfully preventing reinforcements being thrown into the fort, although unable to force an entrance by more or less vigorous attacks, an effort was made to persuade the timid and disaffected residents of the valley to abandon the cause of the patriots and enroll themselves with the King's army in front of Fort Schuyler, by issuing an address signed by Johnson, Claus, and Butler. This document was sent by messengers throughout Tryon County, but it effected little else than to get the messengers themselves in trouble.

About two miles above Fort Dayton (Herkimer) resided a Tory named Shoemaker. Having heard that a clandestine meeting of Tories was to take place at his house, Colonel Weston, the commandant at Fort Dayton, sent a detachment of troops thither. The night was dark and the soldiers were able to surround the house without being discovered, and cautiously concealed themselves until all of the bidden guests were assembled. Among those present

Han Yost Schuyler

were Lieutenant Walter N. Butler and his guard of soldiers and Indians who had accompanied him from St. Leger's camp for the purpose of distributing the inflammatory document, and a number of the disaffected of the county. So complete was the surprise of the attack that Butler was taken while making a speech and his comrades surrendered without bloodshed.

General Arnold at this time was waiting at Fort Dayton for supplies and reinforcements, before marching to the relief of Fort Schuyler. At a court-martial that was immediately convened, with Colonel Willett as judge, Lieutenant Butler and some others were convicted as spies and sentenced to death. At the intercession of some American officers who had been college students with Butler, his life was saved by a reprieve and he was imprisoned at Albany in the common jail. Subsequently he escaped, to lead in the massacre at Cherry Valley.

Among the Tories who were captured and sentenced to death was a half-witted fellow named Han Yost Schuyler. Having been associated with the Indians on the frontier by force of circumstance and inclination, he was regarded by the savages with the superstitious reverence which they have for simple-minded people. His mother, an old half-gypsy creature, and his brother Nicholas implored General Arnold to spare his life, but Arnold was obdurate. She implored passionately and becoming almost frantic in her grief, Arnold proposed terms on which he would grant Han Yost's pardon, his brother Nicholas to be held as hostage for the strict performance of the duties required. He (Han Yost) was to hurry to Fort Schuyler, and so alarm St. Leger's army that he would raise the siege. The half-fool at once accepted the conditions, and it was agreed that his brother Nicholas should forfeit his life if Han Yost should prove recreant or fail to accomplish the duties required of him.

It was also agreed that Thomas Spencer, the Oneida half-breed who had already proved his loyalty and devotion to the cause of the patriots in many ways, should accompany him.

Before they started on their mission the coat and cap of Han Yost were hung up and bullets shot through them, after which preparation, and without arms, they started by different routes towards the Indian camp of St. Leger's army.

Ever since the battle of Oriskany the Indian warriors had been morose and dissatisfied. They had been promised easy success and much plunder, but they had found neither the one nor the other. While they were in the midst of a great pow-wow of dancing, doleful music, and grotesque ceremonies, Han Yost suddenly appeared among them, breathless and with clothes disordered. As he was well known to them, the Indians crowded around him, eagerly questioning him for news from Fort Dayton and the army of General Arnold. He told them that the army was then approaching the fort. When asked, "How many men?" he pointed to the leaves of the forest. When asked how near they were, he showed the fresh bullet holes in his garments. The report spread throughout the camps with amazing rapidity and

Han Yost Schuyler

soon reached headquarters. St. Leger sent for Han Yost, who told the commander a straight and pitiful story; how he had been captured with Walter Butler and others, had been tried and condemned; how on his way to his execution he had broken away from his guards and fled; how shots were fired at him, but he had escaped unharmed although he had had a very narrow escape, as the Colonel could see by his clothes. While this interview was being held Spencer arrived and confirmed the story of Han Yost that the Americans were coming in great force.

Other Oneidas, whom Spencer had seen and posted, followed at intervals from different routes with alarming rumors. One said that Burgoyne's army was cut to pieces, another told St. Leger that Arnold had three thousand men near. The Indians, now thoroughly alarmed, prepared to flee. St. Leger tried every means, by offers of bribes and promises, to induce them to remain, but the panic, and suspicion of foul play, had determined them to go. He tried to make them drunk, but they would not drink. He then besought them to take the rear of his army in retreating; this they refused and indignantly said, "You mean to sacrifice us. When you marched down you said there would be no fighting for us Indians; we might go down and smoke our pipes; whereas numbers of our warriors have been killed, and you mean to sacrifice us also." And notwithstanding the entreaties of Brant, Johnson, and Colonel Claus the council broke up and the Indians fled.

The panic was communicated to the rest of the camp and in a few hours the whole of St. Leger's army was flying in terror toward its boats on Oneida Lake, Han Yost accompanied them in their flight as far as Wood Creek, where he managed to desert, and found his way back to Fort Schuyler that night and was the first to communicate to Colonel Gansevoort the intelligence of Arnold's approach. The Indians, it is said, made themselves merry at the precipitate flight of the whites, who threw away their arms and knapsacks so that nothing should impede their progress. The savages also gratified their passion for murder and plunder by killing many of the white soldiers on the borders of the lake and stripping them of every article of value. They also plundered them of their boats, and according to St. Leger "they became more formidable than the enemy they had to expect." Another account relates that St. Leger, while standing on the border of a swamp alone with Sir John Johnson, reproached the latter with being the cause of the disaffection of the Indians. High words and mutual recriminations followed. Two chiefs, standing ne r, overheard the quarrel, and put an end to it by shouting, "They are coming! They are coming!"

Both officers, terribly alarmed, plunged into the morass. This was a signal for the general retreat of the whole army. Such was their haste that they left their tents, baggage, and artillery behind, and the bombardier was left asleep in the bomb battery! When he awoke he found himself alone, the sole representative of the besieging army. The Indians continued their cry, at intervals, "They are coming! They are coming!" behind the fleeing Tories, and thus amused themselves all the way to Oneida Lake.

Han Yost Schuyler

The retreat of St. Leger from Fort Schuyler and the surrender of Burgoyne at Saratoga brought joy and hope to the harassed settlers of the Mohawk Valley, and except for occasional raids of small bands of Indians along the frontier no further invasion of the British forces was attempted until the summer of 1778.

This year was marked by a series of attacks on the frontier towns of New York and Pennsylvania. In January predatory excursions were made by large bands of Indians and Tories, who made their headquarters at Oghwaga, and of more than a hundred families scattered along the Susquehanna River above Lackawanna not one remained. Then came the destruction of Wyoming and its attendant massacre, followed in quick succession by the destruction of Cobleskill, Andrustown, German Flats, and Cherry Valley, with tales of butchery, torture, and every phase of barbarous cruelty.

An attempt had been made by Congress to secure the good-will of the warriors of the Six Nations, and to accomplish that purpose, if possible, a council of the Six Nations was called in February, 1778, to meet at Johnstown, N. Y. The Indians were so slow or reluctant in assembling that the council was not convened until the 9th of March. It is estimated that nearly seven hundred Indians were present, consisting of Oneidas, Tuscaroras, Onondagas, a few Mohawks, and three or four Cayugas, and not a single Seneca, which tribe was by far the most numerous of all the Iroquois nations. The delegation appointed by the Congress consisted of the Marquis de

Lafayette, Volkert T. Douw and James Duane. The result of the conference was very disappointing to the patriots. Colonel Stone says:

> While the impression at the time seemed to be that the Oneidas, Tuscaroras, and Onondagas would remain neutral and restrain their warriors from taking active part with the British, the commissioners left the council fully persuaded that from the Senecas, Cayugas, and the greater part of the Mohawks, nothing but revenge for their lost friends and tarnished glory at Oriskany and Fort Schuyler was to be expected. Before the year closed it became evident that none but the Oneidas and Tuscaroras were favorable to the cause of the patriots, the Onondagas and Mohawks being as active in the cause of the British as the Senecas and Cayugas. The untiring zeal and energy of Rev. Mr. Kirkland, the missionary stationed among the Oneidas, and the persuasive power of Thomas Spencer, the Oneida half-breed, however, kept the Oneidas and Tuscaroras in line to the end of the war.

During the winter of 1778–79 bands of savages, or Tories disguised as such, kept the inhabitants of the valley in constant fear and alarm, and military men became eager to inaugurate General Washington's plan of carrying the war into the enemy's country. It was known that in the Senecas' country, in the Genesee Valley, and around the lakes of central New York large crops of corn and vegetables and orchards of apples, pears, and small fruits were raised, not alone for the Indians, but as supplies for the British army. It was for the purpose of the destruction of this fair country and the expulsion or extermination of the turbulent tribes that General Sullivan's expedition of 1779 was organized, laid waste the fields and villages of the Senecas and Cayugas and drove the

Sullivan's Expedition 107

inhabitants back to the British frontier posts at Niagara and Oswego.

In April, 1779 (which was previous to the organization of General Sullivan's expedition), General Clinton despatched a portion of Colonel Gansevoort's and Van Schaick's regiments to chastise the Onondagas. The party consisted of five hundred and fifty men under the command of Colonel Van Schaick, who was instructed to burn their castles and villages, destroy their cattle and other property and make as many prisoners as possible. The expedition went down Wood Creek to Oneida Lake, thence up Oswego River to a point on Onondaga Lake, where Salina now stands. As a thick fog concealed their movements they were able to approach within four or five miles before they were discovered. As soon as the first village was attacked, the alarm spread to the others. Three villages, consisting of fifty houses, were destroyed, twelve Indians killed, and thirty-three were made prisoners. A large quantity of corn and beans was consumed and all of the horses and cattle were slaughtered. The councilhouse was not burned, but the swivel therein was spiked and the ancient and, to them, sacred council fire extinguished.

This expedition was cruel and of doubtful wisdom, as it alarmed the neutral Oneidas who were faithful to the Americans, because, having intermarried among the Onondagas, some of their relatives had been either slain or impoverished.

But the ire of the Onondagas was fiercely aroused, not alone on account of the destruction of property and loss of life, but because the great council fire of the confederacy, of which they had been keepers from the organization of the confederacy, had again been extinguished. The fire, in historic times, had been put out by Count Frontenac in 1692, and again extinguished in 1777, and to avenge this, the third extinction, three hundred braves were immediately sent upon the war-path, harassing settlements on both sides of the river. Under the guidance of a Tory they descended upon the German settlement at Cobleskill, murdering, plundering, and burning. The militia turned out, but, being led into an ambuscade, a number of them were killed. They fought bravely and while they were contending with the Indians the people fled in safety to Schoharie. Seven of the soldiers took post in a strong house, which the Onondagas set on fire and the brave young fellows all perished in the flames. The settlement was burned, twenty-two patriots were killed, and forty-two were carried away captives.

While the Indians were doing their deadly work in the vicinity of Cobleskill, another party fell upon the Canajoharie settlement, took three prisoners, captured some horses and drove the people into Fort Plain. On the same day another party attacked a small settlement at Stone Arabia, burned some houses, and killed several people. A party of Senecas also appeared at Schoharie and committed further depredations.

The expedition of General Sullivan into the Senecas' country is, incidentally, of interest to the Mohawk Valley from the fact that the right division of his army

Sullivan's Expedition

under General James Clinton advanced up the Mohawk River with two hundred and ten bateaux and fifteen hundred troops, reaching Canajoharie June 16, 1779, and on June 17th commenced the arduous portage of bateaux and stores to Otsego Lake, twenty miles over exceedingly bad roads. This he accomplished in nine days' time, and on July 1st passed down the lake to its foot, where Cooperstown now stands, and awaited orders. While thus detained scouts were sent out to examine the bed of the outlet of the lake, which constituted the head waters of the Susquehanna River, and found it a narrow, shallow stream half choked with logs and floodwood and not having enough water to float a birch bark Indian canoe. In order to facilitate the passage of loaded bateaux along this rippling forest stream, the troops were ordered to build a substantial log dam across the outlet, by means of which the waters of the lake were raised two feet. On each bank of the Susquehanna wherever a clearing had been found the Indians had planted their crops, while sixty miles below were the Indian village and plantations of Oghwaga.

It was not until August 9th that General Clinton received orders to advance. W. L. Stone says, in his *Life of Brant*

> And when on that day he was relieved from his vexatious halt the dam was broken and his flotilla was not only borne triumphantly along upon the pile of impatient waters, but the swelling of the torrent beyond its banks caused wide and unexpected destruction to the growing crops of the Indians on their plantations and at Oghwaga and its vicinity. They

were moreover greatly affrighted at the sudden and unexpected rise in the waters in the driest season of the year, especially as there had been no rains and the hot midsummer sun was shining from a sky unflecked by fleecy cirrus, undimmed by sombre storm-laden clouds, and attributed the event to the interposition of the "Great Spirit" who thus showed he was angry with them. The country was wild and uninhabited, save by scattered families, and here and there by some few of the more adventurous white settlers in the neighborhood of Unadilla. The sudden swelling of this mountain stream, therefore, bearing upon its surging, tumultuous waters a flotilla of more than two hundred laden vesesls, through a region of primitive forest, was a spectacle which might well appall the untutored inhabitants of the region thus invaded.

At Oghwaga General Clinton was met by a detachment from Paulding's regiment, and on August 22d joined General Sullivan at Tioga Point.

NOTE. Queen Esther, notorious as the "fiend of Wyoming," was living at Sheshequire, six miles below Tioga Point, in 1772, and removed at about that date six miles north and founded a new town, afterward known as Queen Esther's town. This was afterward destroyed by Col. Martley in 1778, when she probably removed to Chemung. She had a son who lost his life a short time previous to the massacre of Wyoming, which was probably the exciting cause of her fury at that place. She was a daughter of French Margaret, granddaughter of Madam Montour, and a sister of Catharine Montour, 2d. She had another sister, Mary, who was the wife of John Cook, *alias* Kanaghargait, a Seneca chief sometimes called White Wings. Her own husband was Eglohawin, chief sachem of the Minsi Delawares.

The Old Klock House, St. Johnsville, N. Y.—1750.

CHAPTER IX

SIR JOHN JOHNSON'S SECOND RAID, OCTOBER, 1780—BATTLE OF STONE ARABIA—BATTLE OF KLOCK'S FIELD—GENERAL ROBERT VAN RENSSELAER—BRITISH ACCOUNT OF THE RAIDS OF CAPTAIN JOSEPH BRANT

DURING the autumn of 1780 the Indians, thirsting for revenge for the wrong and misery inflicted by General Sullivan, were planning extensive expeditions against the Mohawk and Schoharie settlements. The leaders were Sir John Johnson, Brant, and the famous half-breed Corn-Planter. The Indians rendezvoused at Tioga Point, and, ascending the Susquehanna, formed a junction at Unadilla with Sir John Johnson and his forces, which consisted of three companies of his Greens, one company of German Yagers, two hundred of Butler's Rangers, one company of British regulars, under Captain Duncan, and a number of Mohawks. They came from Montreal by way of Oswego, bringing with them two small mortars, a brass three-pounder and a piece called a grasshopper. The plan of invasion was to proceed along the Charlotte River to its source, thence across to the head of the Schoharie, sweep all the settlements along its course to its junction with the Mohawk, and then devastate the beautiful valley down to Schenectady.

How the valley of the Schoharie was devastated, the many tales of cruelty by the Indians and bravery of the white settlers, the dwellings and barns and bountiful harvest that were destroyed, have been told so vividly by J. R. Simms and others that I will not attempt to repeat the gruesome tale at this time; but will endeavor to follow Sir John Johnson and his mixed forces in their progress from Fort Hunter on the Mohawk River, where he arrived October 17th and destroyed everything belonging to the Whigs. On the 18th he began his devastating march up the Mohawk Valley. Caughnawaga was burned and every dwelling on both sides of the river as far west as Fort Plain was destroyed, Sir John advancing with the main body on the south side and Captain Duncan's division on the north. Conspicuous among the sufferers was Jelles Fonda, a faithful and confidential officer under Sir William Johnson, but who, having turned his back upon the royal cause, was singled out as a special mark of vengeance. His mansion at the "Nose" in the town of Palatine was destroyed, together with property estimated at sixty thousand dollars. The Major was absent. Under the cover of a thick fog his wife escaped and made her way on foot to Schenectady, twenty-six miles away.

Sir John encamped, on the 18th, above the "Nose," and on the following morning crossed to the north side at Keder's Riff. A greater part of the motley army continued up the river, destroying crops and buildings, but a detachment of one hundred and fifty men was despatched from Keder's Riff (Spraker's Basin) against the small stockade called Fort Paris,

Sir John Johnson's Second Raid

in Stone Arabia, about two and one half miles from the Mohawk River. This fort was located a few rods northeast of the crossroads of this little hamlet, and at the time mentioned was occupied by Colonel John Brown with a garrison of one hundred and thirty men.

Tidings having been sent to Albany of the advent of Sir John Johnson into the settlements of the Schoharie, General Robert Van Rensselaer, with the Claverack, Albany, and Schenectady regiments, pushed on by forced marches to encounter him, accompanied by Governor Clinton. On the evening of the 17th this body, together with two hundred Oneida Indians, encamped on the Stanton farm in Florida, near the present city of Amsterdam, and from this camp, having heard that Fort Paris was to be attacked on the morning of the 19th inst., he sent word to Colonel Brown to march out and check the advance of Sir John's troops, while at the same time he would be ready to fall on his rear. Brown promptly obeyed and at nine o'clock, the hour designated, marched about half way towards the river and gave battle to Sir John, who had diverted the greater part of his force to meet Colonel Brown at the ruined works of old Fort Keyser. But "the best-laid plans of mice and men gang aft agley," and, as Van Rensselaer's advance was impeded, no diversion was created in Brown's favor. Fort Paris was three miles from the river, and undoubtedly Brown could have defended it successfully against any force that Johnson would have sent against it; and yet, obeying the orders of a general who in other ways that day proved himself to have been incompetent, this brave man met the enemy two thirds of the way to the river, where the contest began. Overpowered by numbers he continued the fight, slowly retreating, expecting every moment to hear the firing in the enemy's rear—but in vain. Contesting the ground inch by inch for some distance, until observing that the Indians were gaining his flank, he ordered a retreat, at which time he received a musket-ball in his breast, killing him instantly. About forty of his men were killed and the remainder sought safety in flight.

Sir John now dispersed his forces in small bands to a distance of five or six miles in every direction to pillage the country. He desolated Stone Arabia, and, proceeding to Klock's field near the present village of St. Johnsville, halted to rest.

General Van Rensselaer was now in close pursuit of Sir John with a strong force, having marched rapidly up the south side of the river, and was joined by Captain McKean with some eighty volunteers, together with a strong body of Oneida warriors, led by their principal chief, Louis Atayatar onghta, who had been commissioned a lieutenant-colonel by Congress. With these additions, the command of Van Rensselaer numbered about fifteen hundred—a force in every way superior to that of the enemy. W. L. Stone in *Life of Brant* says: "Arriving at Keder's ford, General Van Rensselaer found that Sir John had stationed a guard of forty men to dispute his passage. Approaching that point he halted, and did not again advance until the guard of the enemy had been withdrawn. Continuing his march,

Ornamented Window, Church at Stone Arabia.

still on the south side of the river, while the enemy was actively engaged in the work of death and detruction on the north, Van Rensselaer arrived opposite the battle-ground where Brown had fallen, before the firing had ceased, and while the savage war-whoop was yet resounding. This was about 11 A.M., and the Americans came to a halt, about three miles below Garoga Creek, still on the south side. While there, some of the fugitives from Colonel Brown's regiment came running down, and jumping into the river, forded it without difficulty."

As they came to the south bank, the General inquired whence they came. One of them, a militia officer named Van Allen, replied that they had escaped from Brown's battle. "How has it gone?"—"Colonel Brown is killed, with many of his men. Are you going there?" "I am not acquainted with the fording place," said the General. He was answered that there was no difficulty in the case. The General then inquired of Van Allen if he would return as pilot, and the reply was promptly in the affirmative. Hereupon Captain McKean and Louis, the Oneida chief, led their respective commands through the river to the north side, expecting the main army immediately to follow. At this moment Colonel Dubois, of the State levies, rode up to the General, who immediately mounted his horse, and, instead of crossing the river, accompanied the Colonel to Fort Plain, some distance above, to dinner as it was understood. Meantime the baggage-wagons were driven into the river, to serve in part as a bridge for the main body of Van Rensselaer's forces, and they commenced crossing the stream in single files. The passage in this way was not effected until four o'clock P. M., at which time the General returned from Fort Plain and joined them just as the last man had crossed over. Governor Clinton remained at the fort. As the General arrived at the water's edge, Colonel Louis, as the Oneida chieftain was called, shook his sword at him and denounced him as a Tory. Arrived at the north side, Colonel William Harper took the liberty of remonstrating with the General at what he conceived to be a great and unnecessary delay, attended with a needless loss of life and property on the part of the inhabitants who had been suffered thus long to remain unprotected. From that moment Van 'Rensselaer moved with due expedition. The troops were set in motion, and marched in regular order, in three divisions, with the exception of the Oneida warriors and the volunteers under McKean, who regulated their own movements as they pleased—showing no disposition, however, to lag behind. The advance was led by Colonel Morgan Lewis.

Anticipating that he would be compelled to receive an attack, Sir John made his dispositions accordingly. His regular troops, Butler's Rangers, and the Tories less regularly organized, were posted on a small alluvial plain partly encompassed by a sweeping bend of the river. A slight breastwork had been hastily thrown across the neck of the little peninsula thus formed, for the protection of his troops, and the Indians under Thayendanega were secreted among the thick scrub oaks covering the tableland of a few feet elevation;

Sir John Johnson's Second Raid 117

yet farther north a detachment of German Yagers supported the Indians.

It was near the close of the day when Van Rensselaer arrived, and the battle was immediately begun in the open field. Two of the advancing divisions of state troops, forming the left, were directed against the regular forces of Sir John on the flats, beginning their firing from a great distance with small arms only—the field-pieces not having been taken across the river. Colonel Dubois commanded the extreme right, which was so far extended that he had no enemies to encounter. Next to him were McKean's volunteers and the Oneida Indians, whose duty it was to attack Thayendanega's Indians and the Yagers. These were supported by a small corps of infantry commanded by Colonel Morgan Lewis. The Americans' left was commanded by Colonel Cuyler of Albany. Sir John's right was formed of a company of regulars. His own regiment of Greens composed the centre, its left resting upon the ambuscaded Indians. The latter first sounded the war-whoop, which was promptly answered by the Oneidas. Both parties eagerly rushed forward, and the attack for the instant was mutually impetuous.

Dubois, though too far extended, quickly brought his regiment to the support of McKean's volunteers, who were following up the attack of the Oneidas. The hostile Indians manifested a disposition to stand for a few moments; but Dubois had no sooner charged closely upon them than they fled with precipitation to the fording place near the upper Indian castle (Danube), about two miles above—crossing the road in their flight and throwing themselves in the rear of the Greens as a cover. Brant was wounded in the heel, but not so badly as to prevent his escape.

The enemy's regular troops and rangers, however, fought with spirit, although Sir John himself was reported by some to have fled with the Indians. On the flight of the Indians, Major Van Benschoten of Dubois's regiment hastened to the General for permission to pursue the flying enemy. It was just twilight, and the indications were not to be mistaken that the best portion of the enemy's forces were in confusion and on the point of being conquered. The disappointment was therefore great, when, instead of allowing a pursuit of the Indians, or charging upon the feeble breastworks on the flats, and thus finishing the battle, General Van Rensselaer ordered his forces to retire for the night. His avowed object was to obtain a better position for a bivouac, and to renew and complete the battle in the morning—for which he fell back nearly three miles, to Fox's Fort.

Captain McKean and the Oneida chief Louis did not strictly obey orders, and early the next morning started off with their forces in pursuit. Johnson, with the Indians and Yagers, fled toward Onondaga Lake where they had left their boats concealed, his Greens and Rangers following. Van Rensselaer and his whole force pursued them as far as Fort Herkimer, and then McKean and Louis were ordered to press on in advance after the fugitives. They struck the trail of Johnson the next morning and soon afterward came upon his deserted camp with the fires yet burning. Halting for a short time, Colonel Dubois came up and urged them forward, repeating the assurances of the General's near approach and sure support. The Oneida chief shook his head and refused to proceed

Sir John Johnson's Second Raid

another step until General Van Rensselaer should make his appearance. There was accordingly a halt for some time, during which a Doctor Allen arrived from the main army, informing the officer that the pursuit had already been abandoned by the General, who was four miles distant on his return march.

The bitter feeling among the troops and inhabitants of the valley against General Van Rensselaer was intense, and charges of incompetency and even Toryism were freely made. It was even said that owing to family ties he had purposely allowed Sir John to escape from the toils in which the impetuosity of the American troops had surrounded him. However, the General was summoned before a military court and acquitted,—probably with the Scotch verdict "not proven."

It may be of interest to some to read the British reports of these raids as furnished by Guy Johnson:

> Lieut. Clement reports that Captain Brant has effected a very good piece of service and is advancing against the rebel frontier. On his march from hence he came upon the only remaining Indian village of the Oneidas, sixteen miles from Fort Schuyler. He found the village abandoned, but met some Indians who told him they had returned through fear of parties of strange Indians, with many other particulars in which it appeared they had deceived him, for they soon deserted and gave notice to the garrison at Fort Schuyler. Captain Brant then burnt the rebel fort at the village with other buildings and marched to the Indians below Fort Schuyler, where he met the Oneidas in camp and called upon them to follow the example of the rest of their people and return to the British government. About 100 replied that it was their desire and they are now partly come to this place [Niagara].

The small remainder ran towards Fort Schuyler, which they reached, except two, who were shot. [Again:] Lieut. Clement reports that Captain Brant has burnt and destroyed the Oneida village, Conowaroharie, with the rebel fort and village, and retired somewhat to deceive the enemy. They proceeded to the Mohawk River with about 300 Indians and arrived at the settlement called Kley's Barrack about 10 A.M. on August 2d, which having reconnoitred, he and the chief warriors thought proper to detach David Karacanty with the greater part of the Indians to make a detour and suddenly attack Fort Plank [Fort Plain], while Joseph and the remainder should come on directly and prevent any scattering parties from taking shelter in the fort. In this they were disappointed by the too great eagerness of the Indians to take prisoners, who scattered and alarmed the settlement, by which a considerable number of men got into the fort, which made the attack inexpedient, as it was well fortified and had two pieces of cannon mounted. Disappointed they advanced to the upper part of the settlement, where the rebels had a fort at the house of Hendrick Walrod, which they abandoned. This was immediately burned, and scattering, the Indians destroyed the houses till they came to Elias Map's, where they had another picketed fort, which they likewise burned. The extent of the settlement destroyed was on the Mohawk River in length two miles and above five miles in breadth, and containing about 100 houses, two mills, a church, and two forts. They took and killed 300 black cattle and 200 horses, besides hogs, poultry, etc., and destroyed a considerable quantity of grain of different kinds. The number of rebels killed and prisoners amounts to about 45. Captain Brant released a number of women and children and having effected this he retired to Butler's Mills about three days since. With the greater part of the Indians he intends to pay the rebels another visit before their return, for which purpose they have divided into seven parties. These detachments marched by separate routes against German Flats, Schoharie and Cherry Valley, where they took many prisoners, destroyed dwellings, and created intense alarm.

Sir John Johnson's Second Raid

The above report was dated Niagara, Aug. 11, 1780. Again from the British in Sept., 1780:

> Lieut. Col. Butler with 200 rangers and 220 regular troops from the garrison of Niagara was directed to join Sir John Johnson at Oswego and act under his orders. His instructions forbade him to take "a single man, who is not a good marcher and capable of bearing fatigue. I hope Joseph is returned" Governor Haldimand added, "as I would by all means have him employed on this service."

Contrary winds prevented Butler from arriving at Oswego until October 1st, and by that time the garrisons on the Mohawk were warned by their Indian spies (Oneidas) that he had sailed from Niagara on an expedition of some kind. It was not until daybreak on the 17th that the weary column, commanded by Sir John Johnson, passed the fort at the head of the Schoharie, having made a long detour through the wilderness for the purpose of attacking the enemy in an entirely unexpected quarter, and swept along the west bank of that stream down to the Mohawk, burning every building and stack of grain as they went along. Sir John then "detached Captain Thompson of the Rangers and Captain Brant with about 150 Rangers and Indians to destroy the settlement at Fort Hunter on the east side of Schoharie Creek, which they effected without opposition, the inhabitants having fled to the fort." Advancing swiftly up the Mohawk the invaders laid waste the country on both sides until midnight, when utterly exhausted they halted at the narrow pass called the "Nose" to snatch a few hours' sleep. Before daybreak they were again on the march and soon encountered Colonel Brown with 360 (?) men from Stone Arabia, who attempted to check their further progress.'

While the detachments of the 8th and 34th regiments advanced directly upon the front of the enemy's position, Brant with a party of Indians made a circuit through the woods to turn their right flank, and Capt. John Macdonnell led a body of rangers in the opposite direction to turn their left. The position was carried with trifling loss to the assailants, while Colonel Brown and about a hundred of his men were killed or taken.

Johnson reported that:

Captain Macdonnell and Captain Brant exerted themselves on this occasion in a manner that did them honor and contributed greatly to our success. Captain Brant received a flesh wound in the sole of his foot near the former wound.

Before night they were forced to fight a sharp rear-guard action with a pursuing force of more than a thousand men under General Robert Van Rensselaer. They turned upon their assailants, drove them from their position, and crossed the river unmolested. During their raid they had destroyed thirteen grist-mills, many saw-mills, a thousand houses, and about the same number of barns, containing, it was estimated, 600,000 bushels of grain. The severity of the blow from a military point of view was freely acknowledged by their enemies.—CRUIKSHANK.

And this in retaliation for General Sullivan's impolitic expedition into the Indian country.

CHAPTER X

COLONEL MARINUS WILLETT—BATTLE OF DORLACH (SHARON SPRINGS).

DURING the year 1781 small parties of Indians and Tories harassed the settlements of the Mohawk Valley and terrorized the inhabitants. The spirit of the people had in a great measure been crushed, and the militia broken down by the disastrous invasions of the previous year, and no troops seem to have been available for their protection, as the commander-in-chief was again evidently preparing for some enterprise of greater importance than the protection of the valley from the skulking savages of the north.

It was finally decided, however, to consolidate the skeletons of five New York regiments into two, which together with all militia levies were placed in command of Marinus Willett, whose name alone was a tower of strength to the people of Tryon County. A fortnight after his arrival and the gathering of the forces, it was found that his command consisted of barely three hundred men, including officers, with headquarters at Fort Rensselaer (near Fort Plain).

On the 9th of July, 1781, nearly three hundred Indians and a few white men, commanded by a Tory named Doxstader, attacked and destroyed the settlement of Currytown, murdered several of the inhabitants, and carried others away as prisoners. Currytown was a small, straggling village of twenty or thirty houses and situated about three miles from the Mohawk south of the "Nose." One of the houses, that of Henry Lewis, was surrounded by a stockade and used for a fort. The settlers, unsuspicious of danger, were generally at work in the fields when the enemy fell upon them. It was toward noon when the Indians, crouching and crawling, emerged from the forest toward the scattered dwellings and with torch and tomahawk commenced their work of destruction. Among the sufferers were the Dievendorfs, Kellers, Myerses, Bellingers, Tanners, and Lewises. Jacob Dievendorf, the elder, escaped, but his son Frederick was overtaken, tomahawked, and scalped on his way to the fort, and Frederick's brother, a lad of eleven years, was taken prisoner. The enemy plundered all of the barns and dwellings save the fort and a house belonging to a Tory, and either killed or drove away most of the cattle and horses in the neighborhood. When the work of destruction was accomplished the marauders started off in the direction of New Dorlach (now Sharon) with their prisoners and booty.

Colonel Willett was at Fort Plain when Currytown was attacked. On the previous day he had sent out a scout of thirty or forty men under Captain Gross to patrol the country for the twofold purpose of procuring forage and watching the movements of the enemy. They went in the direction of New Dorlach, and when near the present Sharon Springs discovered a portion of the enemy's camp in a cedar swamp. Intelligence of this fact reached Willett at the moment

Colonel Marinus Willett

when a dense smoke, indicating the firing of a village, was seen from Fort Plain in the direction of Currytown. Captain Robert McKean with sixteen men was ordered to that place, with instructions to assemble as many of the militia on the way as possible. With his usual celerity that officer arrived at the settlement in time to assist in extinguishing the flames of some of the buildings yet unconsumed. Colonel Willett, in the meantime, was active in collecting the militia. Presuming that the enemy would occupy the same encampment that night, and being joined by the forces under McKean and Gross, he determined to make an attack upon them at midnight while they were asleep. His whole strength did not exceed one hundred and fifty men, while the enemy's force, as he afterward discovered, consisted of more than double that number.

The night was dark and lowering, and the dense forest that surrounded the swamp encampment of the enemy was penetrated only by a bridle path. His guide lost his way and it was six o'clock in the morning before he came in sight of Doxstader's troops, who, warned of his approach, had taken a more advantageous position. From this position Willett sought to draw them, and for that purpose he sent forward a detachment from the main body, consisting of ten resolute men under Lieutenant Jacob Sammons, to steal as near as possible, give them one well-directed fire, and retreat. The ruse succeeded. Sammons and his men, after discharging their guns with considerable effect, turned their backs at the first yell of the Indians, and the latter sprang forward in pursuit. They were, however, soon met by Colonel Willett in person advancing at the head of the main division, which consisted of one hundred men, while Captain McKean was left with fifty more as reserve, to act as occasion might require, on the right. The Indians did not wait an attack, however, but with great appearance of determination advanced with their wonted shouts and yells, and began to fire.

The onset of the Indians was furious; but they were received with firmness and in turn the Americans advanced with their wonted shouts and such manifestation of spirit as soon caused them to give way. Simultaneously with their attack upon the main body in front, the Indians had made an equally desperate rush upon the right wing, which might have been attended with disaster, but for the destructive fire poured upon them by the reserves of Captain McKean. The Indians, thus driven back, now betook themselves to their old game of firing from behind trees; but Willett's men understood that mode of fighting as well as themselves. They did not, however, practise it long. Willett pressed forward waving his hat and cheering his men, calling out that he could catch in his hat all the balls the enemy might send, and in the same breath exclaiming, "The day is ours!" and with timely and efficient use of the bayonet the whole body of the enemy was put to flight in half an hour after the engagement began. Their camp was taken and their plunder recaptured, and the Indians retreated down their old trail to the Susquehanna. Their loss was severe—nearly forty of their dead being left on the field.

Colonel Marinus Willett

Colonel Willett's loss was five killed and nine wounded. Among the wounded was the brave Captain McKean, who was taken to Fort Plain, where he died a few days after. He received two balls early in the engagement, but kept at his post until it was all over and the Indians had fled, when he collapsed.

Perhaps there is no more heroic figure in the history of the valley during the war of Revolution than that of Colonel Marinus Willett, the intrepid commander of the yeomanry who dispersed the Indians at the battle of Dorlach as related in the foregoing pages. He was born at Jamaica, Long Island, July 31, 1740, being the youngest son of Edward Willett, a farmer in that town. When only eighteen years old he joined the army of General Abercrombie; as a lieutenant in Colonel Delaney's regiment was present at the disastrous battle at Ticonderoga in 1758, and accompanied Bradstreet in his successful expedition against Fort Frontenac the same year. Exposure in the wilderness injured his health, and he was confined by sickness in the newly erected Fort Stanwix until the end of the campaign.

At an early date he became one of the most daring of the "Sons of Liberty" in the city of New York. When the British troops of the New York garrison were ordered to Boston, after the skirmish at Lexington, they attempted, in addition to their own, to carry off a large quantity of spare arms in boxes on wagons. Notwithstanding the remonstrances of Whitehead Hicks, the Tory mayor of New York city, and of Gouverneur Morris and others, Marinus Willett and a small body of the "Sons of Liberty," encouraged by

John Morin Scott, boldly confronted the British soldiers, seized the arms, and carried them back to the now deserted fort. These arms were afterwards used by Gansevoort's regiment, of which Willett was lieutenant-colonel. He was appointed second captain in Colonel McDougal's regiment; accompanied General Montgomery in the expedition against Canada; was appointed to the command of St. John's, where he remained until 1776. In 1777 he was in command of Fort Constitution on the Hudson River opposite West Point, with the rank of lieutenant-colonel. In May of that year he was ordered to Fort Schuyler, where he distinguished himself as the commander of the sortie made from that garrison when the camps of the Indians were destroyed and a large quantity of munitions of war and camp equipage was captured. On August 8th Willett, together with Lieutenant Stockwell, left the fort on a dangerous secret expedition at midnight, skirting the Indians' camp stealthily as Indian scouts, and with the skill of a forest runner evaded the prowling savages. It was raining furiously when they left the sally-port each armed with spear and hunting knife. Between the fort and German Flats, their destination, was an extensive swamp, almost impassable. Notwithstanding this obstruction, the brave fellows crept along the morass on their hands and knees until they reached the river. This they crossed upon a log, using their hands as paddles, and were soon beyond the line of savage sentinels. It was very dark, their pathway was in a thick and tangled woods, and they soon lost their way. The barking of a dog gave indication of proximity to an Indian

Colonel Marinus Willett

camp, and for hours they stood in the water up to their knees, fearing to advance or retreat. The clouds broke away toward dawn and the rain ceased and revealed to them the gruesome evidence that they were on the outskirts of Oriskany's battle-field and near the fatal causeway. With true backwoodsmen's caution they pushed on in a zigzag way, occasionally walking considerable distance in the bed of a stream to foil pursuers that might be on their trail. At last they reached the German Flats in safety, and securing fleet horses hurried down the valley to the headquarters of General Schuyler to urge forward troops for the succor of the garrison of Fort Schuyler.

Returning to the battle of Dorlach: At the time of the attack the Indians had placed most of their prisoners on the horses which they had stolen from Currytown, and each was well guarded. When they were about to retreat before Willett, fearing the recapture of the prisoners and the consequent loss of scalps, the Mohawks began to murder and scalp them. Young Jacob Dievendorf leaped from his horse, and, running toward the swamp, was pursued, knocked down by a blow of a tomahawk on the shoulder, scalped, and left for dead. Willett did not bury his slain, but a detachment of militia, under Colonel Veeder, who repaired to the field after the battle to care for the slain, fortunately discovered and proceeded to bury the bodies of the prisoners who were murdered and scalped near the camp. Young Dievendorf, who was stunned and insensible, had been partially covered with rubbish, when he was seen to move. His bloody face being taken for an

Indian, one of the soldiers levelled his musket to shoot him. A fellow soldier, perceiving his mistake, knocked up his gun and saved the lad's life. He was taken to Fort Plain, and being placed under the care of Dr. Faught, a German physician of Stone Arabia, was restored to health, and lived to be an octogenarian.

Although defeated and driven to the southern frontier, the Tories and Mohawks that comprised the expedition were not long idle, but soon various bands appeared at different points in the Mohawk Valley whose murderous raids met with more or less success in the capture of prisoners, the murder of isolated families, and the destruction of buildings and harvested crops of grain. At the German Flats several spirited encounters took place between the enemy and the patriot militia. Captain Solomon Woodworth and a small band of rangers were drawn into ambush in the vicinity of Fort Dayton, and one of the most desperate and bloody engagements of the war ensued. Woodworth and a large number of his rangers were slain and several prisoners were taken by the Indians. Only fifteen escaped. Another affair occurred at a settlement called Schell's Bush, about four miles northeast of Herkimer village. "The heroic defence of one Christian Schell is related in stirring prose and halting verse." Schell or Shell was a wealthy German, and, in order to protect his family and his extensive farm buildings, erected a strong block-house of stout logs, of two stories, the upper one projecting so as to allow the inmates to fire perpendicularly upon the assailants. No windows

Colonel Marinus Willett

were built in the first story, but loopholes were placed on all sides in order to reach all points of attack, the entrance being protected by a massive door of hewn logs strongly bolted and barred. In constant fear of incursions of hostiles, Schell kept his diminutive castle well supplied with ammunition, water, and food. One sultry day in August, 1781, while the people were generally in the field, Donald McDonald, one of the Scotch refugees from Johnstown, with a party of sixty Mohawk Indians and Tories, made a descent upon Schell's Bush. With the command were two noted traitors named Empie and Casseleman.

The inhabitants mostly fled to Fort Dayton for safety, but Schell and his family took refuge in his block-house. He and his two sons were at work in the fields. The two sons were captured, but the father and the four other boys, who were near, succeeded in reaching the block-house in safety. The small fort was soon invested, but the assailants were kept at a respectful distance by the fire from the garrison. Schell's wife loaded the muskets, while her husband and sons discharged them with sure aim.

McDonald tried to burn the block-house, but was unsuccessful. Procuring a crowbar he boldly ran up to the door and attempted to force it. After striking a few powerful blows with the bar, he was fired on by Schell and wounded so severely in the leg that he fell to the ground near the entrance. Quickly unbarring the door, Schell pulled the Scotchman into the block-house, a prisoner, at the same time securing his gun. Being well supplied with ammunition his capture enabled the besieged patriots to continue the vigorous defence, which kept the assailants at a safe distance or under cover of trees, stone walls and outlying buildings. At the capture of the Tory leader the battle ceased for a time. Schell was confident that the enemy would not attempt to burn his castle while their leader was a prisoner therein, and taking advantage of the lull in the battle he went into the second story and composedly sang the favorite hymn of Luther, "A firm fortress is our Lord, a good defence and Weapon."

But the respite was short, for the Indians, maddened at the loss of several of their number, and their commander prisoner, rushed up to the fort on all sides, and five of them succeeded in thrusting the muzzles of their pieces through the loopholes.

Mrs. Schell, a vigorous, quick-witted woman, seized an axe and with well-directed blows ruined every musket by bending the barrels. At the same time Schell and his sons kept up a brisk fire, killing some, wounding others, and finally drove the enemy to cover again.

In the dusk of the August twilight, Schell ran up to the second story and calling his wife in a loud voice told her that Captain Small's troops were approaching from Fort Dayton, and in a few minutes he shouted in a still louder voice: "Captain Small, march your company round upon this side of the house." "Captain Getman, you had better wheel your men to the left and come up on that side."

There were, of course, no troops approaching, but the enemy, deceived by the strategem, fled to the

Lady Johnson, "Lovely Polly Watts," Wife of Sir John Johnson, Bart.

woods. McDonald was taken to Fort Dayton the next day, where his leg was amputated, from which operation he died in a few hours. The intrepid Schell and his brave family clung to their post which they had so well and skilfuly defended. The two sons were carried away to Canada, from whence they returned after the war. They asserted that nine of the wounded died on the retreat.

The loss of the enemy around the block-house was eleven killed and six wounded. None of the defenders of this little frontier castle were injured.

At a subsequent day, Schell, being at work in a field with two of his sons, at no great distance from the fort, was fired upon by a party of Mohawks concealed in the standing wheat. He was severely wounded and one of his sons killed. The old man was taken to the fort, where he died of his wound.

Many tales are told of murders and hair-breadth escapes from marauding Mohawks during the summer and autumn of 1781, but the activity of the brave Willett and the tireless energy of bands of patriotic rangers soon cleared the valley of hostiles and allowed the farmers to resume the cultivation of farms which they had been obliged to abandon.

CHAPTER XI

LADY JOHNSON

LADY Mary Watts Johnson, the wife of Sir John Johnson, is, in memory, a picturesque personality that hovers amid the stirring scenes of the Revolution that were enacted around her old home, Fort Johnson, on the Mohawk.

She was a scion of a family of old New York whose ancestors were among the makers of that lordly city, and whose descendants have filled many positions of trust and honor in commerce, literature, and statecraft, on the battle-fields, and in the legislative halls of the nation. She came, in 1773, as a bride to the home of her husband, a beautiful young girl of nineteen fresh from the glitter and wealth of the fashionable society of New York and the post-nuptial feasts and entertainments at Albany and Schenectady.

The voyage of the bridal party up the Hudson was almost equivalent, in point of duration, to a voyage to Europe at the present day, occupying, as it did, about six or eight days.

We can imagine that the sloop was selected with care and that much thought was bestowed upon the arrangement of the cabin and the necessary stocking of the larder with wines and the delicacies of the season. The party consisted of Sir John, Lady John-

Lady Johnson

son, and her brother, Stephen Watts, and probably a maid for the lady, and servants for the gentlemen. If they were very much in love with each other or at all romantic, they must have looked forward with pleasure to this week of idleness in which to enjoy each other's presence untrammelled by the requirement of social feasts and functions on shore.

Washington Irving has given a description of a voyage up the Hudson under the white wings of early days:

> What a time of intense delight was the first sail through the highlands. I sat on deck as we slowly tided along at the foot of those stern mountains, and gazed with wonder and admiration at cliffs impending far above me crowned with forests, with eagles sailing and screaming around them; or listened to the unseen streams dashing down precipices; or beheld rock and tree and cloud and sky reflected in the glassy stream of the river. And then how solemn and thrilling the scene as we anchored at night at the foot of these mountains clothed with overhanging forests; and everything grew dark and mysterious; and I heard the plaintive note of the whip-poor-will from the mountain-side, or was startled now and then by the sudden leap and splash of the sturgeon.

From Schenectady the journey of the bridal party was not made in a palatial railroad coach of the twentieth century, but on a rude Mohawk River flatboat propelled by a half-score of half-naked polemen into the heart of the wilderness, into the Mohawks' country.

Have you ever imagined the feelings of this young bride as she contemplated the environment of her new home, and contrasted it with the social pleasures with which she was surrounded at her home in the metropolis?

It is true that the stone baronial mansion, rising grim and gray from the midst of a grove of young locust, was imposing in size and appearance, and its environs pleasing to a lover of nature.

Thirty paces to the east a forest stream ran gurgling and seething through the grounds, and, two hundred paces to the south, lost itself in the flood of the Mohawk. The high grounds immediately to the north had been cleared of forest growths, but the ravine through which the Kayaderosseros Creek flowed was dark and damp under the shade of towering pines and rank undergrowth. Stretching to the east and to the west, on both sides of the river, was a long, narrow line of fertile flats, a section of the great granary of the Mohawk which the stream with its silvery glint cut in twain. The building itself seemed to wear an air of hospitality, which was even more apparent when the portal was crossed.

The interior of the house was finished with panelled walls and wide heavy mouldings, each of its eight rooms being of generous size. A wide hall on the main floor, with its stairway guarded by a narrow mahogany rail and slim baluster, was repeated above, while the stairs continued on to the large garret with huge beams and dormer windows.

The store which formerly flanked the building on the west side, but a little in front, had been removed, but the two smaller stone buildings, one on each side of the house, for kitchen and servants' quarters, still remained. Back of the house, just at the entrance of the high grounds of the ravine through which the stream flowed, stood the grist-mill, with flume leading

The East Room, Old Fort Johnson.

to the dam a few hundred feet to the north, while on the left bank of the creek were barns, storehouses, and one or two dwellings.

Of the domestic affairs at the mansion we know nothing, but it is assumed, that, with wealth at his command, Sir John's retinue of servants must have been ample and the regime adequate.

It is said that Lady Johnson was accompanied by her brother, Stephen Watts, and that frequent visits to friends at Schenectady and Albany relieved somewhat the monotony of her existence.

It is true that the Hall was but ten miles away, but what sort of companionship would Molly Brant and her brood of half-savage half-breeds afford to a young girl fresh from the pleasures of the social life of the city and the fond care of parents, relatives, and friends? Before the end of a twelvemonth, death invaded the Hall at Johnstown, and left vacant a space in the life of Tryon County and the home life of Sir William that Sir John was called upon to attempt to fill. How inadequate his attempt and how futile his endeavor history records.

How long Molly Brant and her children remained at the Hall I have no means of knowing, but it is probable that it was for a number of months or perhaps a year; but it is safe to assume that she went with Guy Johnson, Brant, and the Mohawks when they disappeared in the Indian country in August, 1775, as she is known to have been living at Joseph Brant's home at Indian Castle previous to active hostilities in the Mohawk Valley; was at Saratoga with the Mohawks previous to the surrender of Burgoyne; and went to Niagara with the Indians during Sullivan's raid in 1779. She died in 1805, presumably at Niagara, but up to the present time no knowledge of her burial place can be obtained.

Nevertheless, Lady Johnson lived at Johnson Hall, Johnstown, after Sir William's death, doing the honors as hostess and mingling in the society of that frontier village. The family of John Butler lived about two miles south of Johnstown and were intimate friends and frequent visitors at the Hall, Walter N. Butler, the son of John Butler, being a close friend of the new Baronet, and a comrade in the subsequent raids through the valley which made their names notorious in history, and, in the case of Lieutenant Walter N. Butler, infamous.

Mention has been made in a previous chapter of the removal of Lady Johnson from the Hall by Colonel Dayton immediately after the exodus of Sir John and his Highlanders and their fearful march through the Adirondack wilderness, at which time she was taken to Albany, nominally under arrest. Here she remained some time, until it was discovered that she was in communication with Sir John in Canada, giving him valuable information detrimental to the cause of the patriots, when she was removed and placed under closer surveillance.

It is said, and it is conceded to be true, that Lady Johnson was held as a hostage for the good behavior of her husband, and that she was threatened by the officer in charge in the following terms:

"My command does not extend beyond this province; but if Sir John comes one foot within my district with his murderous allies—*your fate is sealed!*" "How, sir, what do you mean? What can I do?" gasped the lady. "I mean, madam, that if your husband lets his Indians go on scalping our people, we cannot prevent them from shooting *you.* . . . Your case is different from all others. Sir John has power over the Indians whom no one else can control. We have no wish to injure you individually; but we must save our people from his savages. *We hold you and your children as hostages.*"

If such language was used to a delicate, helpless woman, it was certainly brutal, but it is also true that no such action would or could have been enforced, and the threat must be considered as the vaporing of an irresponsible mind. No one supposes for a moment that General Washington or General Schuyler would permit a woman, however high or however lowly her station, to suffer for the acts of her husband.

Lady Johnson at this time was undoubtedly an irritable, petulant woman (made so perhaps by her delicate condition), imbued with a very exalted idea of her station as the wife of a baronet of the realm of Great Britain, and, because she was restrained from communicating with Sir John while within the lines of the patriots, she rebelled and resented the restraint that was accorded to the wives and families of the Tories of the valley who were fighting in the ranks of the British troops.

In January, 1777, Lady Johnson made her escape from her captors, in disguise "through deepest snow, through extreme cold weather, through lines of ingrates and enemies, into the loyal city of New York."

The following incidents of her escape are related by her daughter-in-law, Mrs. Christopher Johnson:

Having obtained passes, the party, which consisted of Lady Johnson, her maid, three children, and Tony, an old family slave, fled in disguise. The children were, probably, William, born in 1775, a little daughter born in 1776, and an infant born during her captivity and at the time of her escape (?) not many weeks old. Horses and a sleigh had been secured and they proceeded on their way without obstruction, except that they were occasionally obliged to show their passes until they were in the vicinity of Grove house, which was only a short distance from the British lines. Here, under some cattle sheds, they left their equipage, without going to the house, and made their way towards the Hudson. Travelling all day, each one carrying a child, they were fortunate in finding a resting place towards evening, where they received food and shelter, but the infant, who had to obtain its nourishment from its mother's breast, suffered from the physical exhaustion of my lady and became a source of great anxiety.

They arose in the morning, however, to find that they were only two miles from the river, but the problem of crossing could only be solved at its banks. Hurrying forward with all speed to escape a Continental soldier who they understood was hunting for the party, they reached the river only to find that the ice was breaking up and floating down the stream in great masses, occasionally leaving openings between. The centre of the river seemed to be comparatively clear, and if a boat could be secured, and they could take advantage of an opening between the cakes and get through to the open water before the masses of ice came together, they stood a fair chance in reaching the opposite bank of the river.

A boat and boatman was fortunately found and by the use of gold, of which Lady Johnson had a good supply, the man agreed to make the attempt. Clasping her infant closely in her arms to give it warmth, its little chilled face and closed eyes giving her great anxiety, she watched Tony's guidance of the boat with fear and trembling until they were at last in midstream, clear of the threatening masses of ice, and in half an hour reached the opposite shore.

The British tents were in sight; gold was thrown to the

boatman, and though the snow was deep and soft the lady, staggering with weakness, struggled through the mile which yet separated them from the first line of sentries. Indians were the first who spied the party, and, though they received with their usual composure the announcement of the lady's name, a glance sent off two of their number towards the camp while the others, wrapping some furs around the lady and her infant, lifted them with the utmost care and tenderness in their powerful arms, till they were met by the messenger returning with blankets and mattresses hastily formed into litters. On these all were carefully deposited and carried on swiftly, Tony weeping in joy and thankfulness over his mistress and trying to comfort her by telling her that Sir John was coming.

The poor mother cast one hopeful glance toward the distance, and another of anxiety upon her infant, who just opened its little eyes, and ere she could see that it was the last convulsion of the sinking frame she was clasped in the arms of her husband and was borne, insensible, to the quarters of the commander-in-chief, where every care and comfort was bestowed upon her and her children that their exhausted state required.

The first delight of being restored to her husband and seeing her children at rest and in safety was marred by the anguish of missing the little loved one whom she had borne through so much sorrow and suffering. "But a few hours sooner," she thought, "and my pretty one had been saved." But the joy and thankfulness of those around her soon stilled her repining. Both her surviving children appeared to be entirely restored to health; but with the little girl the appearance was fallacious. After the first week her strength and appetite declined, and her parents had the grief of laying her in an untimely grave, from the destructive effects of cold and exposure on a frame previously debilitated by illness during her mother's captivity, when she could not procure either advice or proper medicines.

After a short stay in New York city Sir John

returned to Canada, and from that time until the close of the war his energy was devoted to strenuous aggression against the inhabitants of the territory of his birthplace. Subsequently Lady Johnson joined her husband in Canada, her principal dwelling place being in Montreal, although the summer months were spent, frequently, on Sir John's seigniory at Argenteuil on the Ottawa River. She also visited in England, where she was much admired in court circles. Lady Johnson bore her husband ten sons and four daughters. One son, James Stephen Johnson, was killed at the siege of Badajoz, in 1814: one daughter, Catherine Maria Johnson, married Major-General Bernard Foord Bowes, who fell at Salamanca, in 1812, while leading the troops to an assault. A public monument was erected to his memory in St. Paul's Cathedral, London. Lady Johnson died in Montreal August 7, 1815. Her husband survived her, and died in the same place, January 4, 1830. Both are buried at "Mount Johnson," near Chambly, Province of Quebec. (General J. Watts de Peyster's *Sir John Johnson.*)

Much has been written about the first raid of Sir John Johnson in 1780, which is said to have been undertaken not alone in revenge for the alleged cruelty to his wife and the death of two of his children through the hardships and exposure incident to Lady Johnson's escape through the American lines to the city of New York, but also for the sordid reason of regaining his buried treasures and papers left behind in his flight through the Adirondacks in 1776. These

Lady Johnson 143

treasures consisted of a large quantity of plate and other valuables together with papers and documents whose intrinsic value is not known. The plate was undoubtedly of great value, as it is said that it was packed in the knapsacks of forty soldiers.

Without doubt other valuable plate was also removed to Canada at the same time by the Mohawks. Upon their first flight from the valley the communion service and paraphernalia of Queen Anne's Chapel at Fort Hunter, given to the Mohawks in 1712, was placed in a hogshead and buried on the Hudson farm west of the mouth of the Schoharie River. This plate was dug up uninjured, but the more destructible ornaments of the altar were destroyed. The plate is now in the custody of the descendants of Joseph Brant at Brantford and Deseronto, Ontario, Canada, in an excellent state of preservation, an almost fabulous value being placed upon it.

Whether the Johnsons' valuables were placed in hogsheads or chests we do not know, as the faithful slave who was left behind to watch over and guard the secret place of burial was true to his trust, although he became the property of an American upon the flight of Sir John, and returned to Canada with him at the time of its removal. The route taken was north from Johnstown to Sacandaga River, thence to the Hudson and Scroon rivers, to Scroon Lake and Lake Champlain, via Crown Point to Canada. It is said, however, that this plate, which was handled by hands imbued with blood of the Vischers, the Putmans, the Fondas, and other residents of the old town of Caughnawaga, was never destined to be of any profit to Sir John, for the papers and documents were destroyed through dampness and, "the silver and other articles retrieved at such a cost of peril, of life, of desolation, and of suffering, was not destined to benefit any one. What, amid fire and sword and death and devastation, had been recovered was placed on shipboard for conveyance to England, and by the irony of fate the vessel foundered in the gulf of St. Lawrence, and its precious though blood-stained freight sank into the abyss of the sea."

With Sir John Johnson's second raid, in October of the same year, 1780, his mission of vengeance ended, although he still continued to be a "menace" to the northern frontier.

It is said that the history of one century should be written by the people of the next. It is now a century and a quarter later than the period of Sir John Johnson's raids of vengeance. What is the verdict of its historians? Are the people of old Tryon County ready to rehabilitate the man whose war-cry was vengeance, whose instruments of death were the scalping-knife, the tomahawk, and the torch, inflicted for the loss of wide domains and for fancied indignities to his young wife? Was it for love of old England, of which he was an alien, that he refused to sign a pledge and keep his parole? His conduct at Oriskany and Fort Schuyler was legitimate, heroic warfare, and if he had continued to meet the American soldiers face to face and trusted to the God of battles to decide, we might attribute his zeal to loyalty to the King and love of the fatherland; but the desolation of fair fields, the burning of granaries, the sacking of homesteads, the failure to

Major Stephen Watts

restrain the hands that carried the torch and the scalping-knife, be those hands red or white, can never be condoned in one century or many.[1]

THE WOUNDING OF MAJOR STEPHEN WATTS

Mention has been made of the serious and almost fatal wounding of Major Stephen Watts, the brother of Lady Polly Watts Johnson. As Major Watts was a guest of Sir John at Fort Johnson and Johnson Hall it is probable that he fled to Canada through the Adirondack wilderness with Sir John Johnson and his Scotch retainers in May, 1776, although it is possible that he may have gone with Colonel Guy Johnson when he disappeared in the Indian country in May, 1775.

However, in July, 1777, we find him with St. Leger's army in front of Fort Schuyler, and in command of the second detachment of "Johnson's Greens" at the battle of Oriskany, August 6, 1777. This body of soldiers was comprised almost entirely of Tories who had fled from the valley with the Johnsons, and now returned as British subjects to fight for the King and to regain, if possible, the lands and homesteads they had abandoned.

Stories of heroism in battle, although accompanied with a display of brutal passions, often engage the attention of the most gentle of readers at their recital, causing them to forget for the time being the barbarity of war, and constraining them to rejoice in a victory which has all the elements of beastly conflict.

[1] Since the above was put in print it has been ascertained through the inspection of the Archives of the province of Ontario, that Sir John Johnson received from the British Government $221,000 for his losses by confiscation and sequestration after the War of Revolution.

Such I think is the case with that part of the engagement which relates to the fratricidal combat between the Americans and Major Watts's detachment of "Johnson's Greens," which resulted in victory for the patriots.

This part of the Oriskany engagement has always fascinated me, and the old proverb, "When Greek meets Greek then comes the tug of war," seems peculiarly apt when applied to that gruesome contest.

It was at the time of the cessation of that terrific thunder-storm which drenched friend and foe alike and caused even the Indians to scurry to cover like a covey of partridges, and the Americans were fighting with a fury that was slowly but surely turning the tide of battle in their favor, that the troops of Major Watts dashed forward against the ranks of the nearly exhausted but still fearless Americans. As they drew near it was observed by this patriotic band that they were former neighbors, and in some cases relatives, who had fled from old Tryon County with the Johnsons and now returned with arms in their hands and bitter hate in their hearts. After the first discharge of their muskets the recognition seemed mutual, as with a snarl and howl of rage they leaped upon each other with the fierceness of tigers. Clubbing their muskets, or discarding them entirely, they drew their knives and grappled each other, or throttled with bare hands, sometimes dying together in one another's close embrace.

It was a terrible struggle, exhibiting all of the cruelty and brutality which distinguishes civil war in all its gruesome details.

Major Stephen Watts

It was in this fierce combat that Major Watts was wounded, about the time that the Indians raised the retreating cry "Oonah! Oonah!" and fled, the Tories soon following them, leaving their dead and wounded to the care of the victorious though sadly stricken Americans.

Mrs. Bonney, according to Colonel W. L. Stone, gives the following account of the wounding and subsequent rescue of the Major.

Major Watts was wounded through the leg by a ball and in the neck by a thrust from a bayonet which passed through the back of the windpipe and occasioned such an effusion of blood as to induce not only him but his captors to suppose (after leading him two or three miles) that he must die in consequence. He begged his captors to kill him; they refused and left him by the side of a small stream under the shade of a bridge, where he was found two days subsequently, his wound in bad condition, but still alive. He was borne by some Indians to Schenectady, where his leg was amputated, and where he remained until sufficiently recovered to bear a voyage to England.

It is said on the authority of General de Peyster, his grand-nephew, that soon after his arrival in England he married a Miss Nugent, and lived and died in elegant retirement surrounded by a noble family of equally brave sons.

J. R. Simms gives some additional details of the finding of the desperately wounded Major:

Being discovered by Henry N. Failing, a private soldier of the Canajoharie district, he kindly carried him to a little stream, that he might slack his thirst and die more easily. To his thanks for his kindness he added the gift of his watch, a silver-cased one, and of a style known at that period as a "bull's-eye" from its resemblance in shape. Two days after, Major Watts was discovered alive by some straggling Indians. . . . The subsequent history of this watch was as follows: Not long after he obtained it, Failing sold it to a Marten G. Van Alstyne for $300 Continental money (value at that time about $30), who retained it in his possession during his lifetime. What finally became of this relic of that bloody field is unknown.

CHAPTER XII

WILL OF SIR WILLIAM JOHNSON

IN the name of God, amen—I, Sir William Johnson, of Johnson Hall, in the county of Tryon and Province of New York, Bart., being of sound and disposing mind, memory and understanding, do make, publish and declare, this to be my last will and testament, in manner and form following:

First and principally, I resign my soul to the great and merciful God who made it, in hopes, through the merits alone of my blessed Lord and Saviour, Jesus Christ, to have a joyful resurrection to life eternal; and my body I direct to be decently interred in the place which I intend for it; and I would willingly have the remains of my beloved wife, Catharine, deposited there, if not done before my decease; and I direct and desire my hereinafter mentioned executors to provide mourning for my housekeeper, Mary Brant, and for all her children; also for young Brant and William, both half-breed Mohawks, likewise my servants and slaves; it is also my desire that the sachems of both Mohawk villages be invited to my funeral, and there to receive each a black stroud blanket, crape and gloves, which they are to wear, and follow as mourners, next after my own family and friends. I leave it to the discretion of my executors, to get such of my friends and acquaintances for bearers as they shall judge most proper, who are to have white scarves, crapes and gloves, the whole expense not to exceed three hundred pounds currency. And as to the worldly and temporal estate, which God was pleased to endow me with, I devise, bequeath and dispose of in the following manner: Imprimis. I will, order and direct, that all such just debts as I may owe, at the time of my decease, together with my funeral expenses of every kind, to be paid by my son, Sir John Johnson, Bart. Item. I give and bequeath to the following persons the sums of money hereafter mentioned, which several sums of money are to be paid to them, by my executors, out of the money I may have in the three per cent. consolidated annuities, of which the heir of the late Sir William Baker has the management, and that in six months after my decease. And first, to the children of my present housekeeper, Mary Brant, the sum of one thousand pounds sterling, to wit: To Peter, my natural son by said Mary Brant, the sum of three hundred pounds sterling, and to each of the rest, being seven in number, one hundred pounds each; the interest thereof to be duly received and laid out to the best advantage by their guardians or trustees, and also the income of whatever other legacies, &c., as are hereafter to be mentioned, until they come of age or marry, except what is necessary for their maintenance and education. Item. To young Brant, *alias* Keghneghtaga, and William, *alias* Tegcheunto, two Mohawk lads, the sum of one hundred pounds York currency to each or the survivor of them.

After paying the before mentioned sums of money, I bequeath to my dearly beloved son, Sir John Johnson, the remaining part of what money I may then have left in the before mentioned, and the other half to be equally divided between my two sons-in-law, Daniel Claus and Guy Johnson, for the use of their heirs. Item. I bequeath to my son, Sir John Johnson, my library and household furniture at the Hall, except what is in my bedroom and in the children's rooms or nursery, which is to be equally divided among them; I also bequeath to him all my plate, except a few articles which I gave to the children of my housekeeper, Mary Brant; he is also to have one-fourth part of all my slaves, and the same of my stock of cattle of every kind. To my two daughters, Ann Claus and Mary Johnson, two-fourths of my slaves and stock of cattle; the other fourth of my slaves and stock of cattle of every kind, I give and bequeath to the children of Mary Brant, my housekeeper, or to the survivors of them,

The Doorway, Old Fort Johnson.

Will of Sir William Johnson

to be equally divided amongst them, except two horses, two cows, two breeding cows, and four sheep, which I would have given before any division is made to young Brant and William of Canajoharie, and that within three months after my decease. I also give and devise all my own wearing apparel, woolen and linen, &c., to be equally divided among the children of my said housekeeper, Mary Brant, share and share alike.

In the next place I dispose of my real estate, all of my own acquiring, in the following manner, and as I maturely weighed the affair, and made the most equitable division which my conscience directed, I expect all who share of it will be satisfied, and wish they may make a proper use of it. And first, to my son, Sir John Johnson, Bart., I devise and bequeath all my estate at and about Fort Johnson, with all the buildings, improvements, &c., thereunto belonging, to be, by him and his heirs, forever peaceably possessed and enjoyed. Also a small tract of land on the south side of the river, opposite Fort Johnson; fifty thousand acres of Kingsland or Royal Grant, all in one body, except the few lots which I have otherwise disposed of; also my share in a patent called Klock & Nellis, jr., on the north side of the Mohawk River. I also devise and bequeath to my son, Sir John Johnson, all my right and title to the Salt Lake, Onondaga, and the lands around it, two miles in depth, for which I have a firm deed, and it is also recorded in the minutes of council at New York; I likewise devise and bequeath to my said son lot No. 10 in said meadow or patent Sacandaga, containing two hundred and sixty-three acres, to be by him and his heirs, of his body lawfully begotten, forever quietly and peaceably possessed and enjoyed; lastly, I do most earnestly recommend it to my son to show lenity to such of the tenants as are poor and be of upright conduct in all his dealings with mankind, which will, upon reflection, afford more satisfaction and heart-feeling pleasure, to a noble and generous mind, than the greatest opulency.

In the next place, I devise and bequeath to my son-in-law, Colonel Daniel Claus, and to his heirs, the tract of land whereon he lives, to wit: from Dove kill to the creek which lies about four hundred yards to the northward of the new dwelling house of Colonel Guy Johnson, together with all the islands thereto belonging; also the house and lots in Albany which I purchased of Henry Holland, together with the water lot adjoining thereto, which I purchased of the corporation of Albany, together with all the buildings and other improvements thereon.

I further devise and bequeath unto the said Daniel Claus and the heirs of his body, all my right in the patent adjoining the German Flats, on the south side of the Mohawk River, containing about sixteen hundred acres; also three lots in the patent of Kingsborough, to wit: No. thirteen, fourteen and fifty-seven; in the western allotment of three lots in Sacandaga patent, to wit: No. twenty-nine, sixty-six, and twenty-seven, containing each two hundred and fifty acres; a third part of a lot in Schenectady, which exchanged with Daniel Campbell, Esq.; also ten thousand acres of land in the Royal Grant, next to that of Sir John Johnson, which is never to be sold or alienated. And lastly, I devise and bequeath unto the said Daniel Claus and the heirs of his body, nine hundred acres, the half of that land that was Gilbert Tice's, in the nine partners patent, between Schoharie and the Mohawk; the whole of the several tracts, lots and houses and before mentioned, to be by him and his heirs, of his body lawfully begotten, forever quietly and peaceably possessed and enjoyed. Item. I devise and bequeath to my son-in-law, Colonel Guy Johnson, and the heirs of his body lawfully begotten, the farm and tract of land whereon he now lives, together with all the islands, buildings, and other improvements thereon; also the house and lot of land in Schenectady, purchased by me of Paul Cowes, and now in the possession of the said Guy Johnson; all my right in the Northampton patent, which I purchased of one Dewey; two lots in Sacandaga patent containing one thousand acres, to wit: lot No. one and two, near to the river and on both sides of Sacandaga Creek; three lots of land in Kingsborough, No. eighty-seven, eighty-eight and eighty-nine, containing each one hundred acres of land,

A Door at Old Fort Johnson.

and one in the eastern allotment; ten thousand acres of land in the Royal Grant, now called Kingsland, adjoining to the ten thousand acres given to Colonel Daniel Claus, which is never to be sold nor alienated on any account; and lastly, nine hundred acres in the half of that land which was Gilbert Tice's in the nine partners patent between Schoharie and the Mohawk village; all the above-mentioned farms, tracts of land and houses with their appurtenances, to be by him and his heirs, of his body lawfully begotten, forever peaceably and quietly possessed and enjoyed. I devise and bequeath unto Peter Jackson, my natural son by Mary Brant, my present housekeeper, the farm and lot of land which I purchased from the Snells in the Stoneraby patent, with all the buildings, mill and other improvements thereon; also two hundred acres of land adjoining thereto, being part of Kingsborough patent, to be laid out in a compact body, between the Garoge and Caniadutta Creeks; also four thousand acres in the Royal Grant, now called Kingsland, next to the Mohawk River, and another strip or piece of land in the Royal Grant, from the Little Falls or carrying-place to lot No. one, almost opposite the house of Hannicol Herkimer, and includes two lots, No. three and No. two, along the river side, and which are now occupied by Ury House &c. I devise and bequeath unto Elizabeth sister of the aforesaid Peter, and daughter of Mary Brant, all that farm and lot of land in Harrison's patent, on the north side of the Mohawk River, at No. nineteen, containing near seven hundred acres, bought by me several years ago of Mr. Brown, of Salem, with all the buildings and appurtenances thereunto belonging; also two thousand acres of land in the Royal Grant, now called Kingsland, and that to be laid out joining to that of her brother Peter, both which she and the heirs of her body, lawfully begotten, are to enjoy peaceably forever.

To Magdalene, sister of the two former, and daughter of Mary Brant, I devise and bequeath that farm near to Anthony's Nose, No. eight, containing about nine hundred acres of land, and on which Mr. Broat now lives, with all the buildings and improvements and other appurtenances thereunto belonging; also two thousand acres of land in the Royal Grant, now called Kingsland, adjoining to that tract of her sister Elizabeth.

To Margaret, sister of the above named Magdalene, and daughter of Mary Brant, I devise and bequeath two lots of land, part of Stoneraby patent, the one to wit: No. twenty-five, which I bought of William Marshall, contains one hundred acres, the other, No. twelve, contains one hundred and thirty-one acres and a half, or thereabouts, which I purchased of Peter Weaver; also two thousand acres in the Royal Grant, now called Kingsland, to be laid out next to her sister Magdalene.

To George, my natural son by Mary Brant, and brother to the four before-mentioned children, I devise and bequeath two lots of land, part of Sacandaga patent, known by Nos. forty-three and forty-four, and called New Philadelphia, containing two hundred and fifty acres each; also a small patent or tract of land called John Braekans, lying on the north side of the Mohawk River, almost opposite to the Canajoharie castle, and contains two hundred and eighty acres or thereabouts; and lastly, three thousand acres in the Royal Grant, now called Kingsland, next to the two thousand acres given to his sister Margaret. The said farms or tracts of land with all the buildings and other appurtenances belonging to them, are to be by him, and the heirs of his body lawfully begotten, forever quietly and peaceably possessed and enjoyed.

To Mary, daughter of Mary Brant, and sister of the before-mentioned five children, I devise and bequeath two thousand acres in the Royal Grant, now called Kingsland, adjoining those of her brother George; also two lots in Stoneraby patent, No. thirty-six and thirty-eight, containing about one hundred and fifty acres, which I bought of Peter Davis and Hannes Kilts.

To Susannah, daughter of Mary Brant and sister of the foregoing six children, I devise and bequeath three thousand acres of the Royal Grant, now called Kingsland, laid out adjoining to them of her sister Mary.

To Anne, sister of the foregoing seven children by Mary

The Hall, Old Fort Johnson.

Will of Sir William Johnson 155

Brant, I devise and bequeath three thousand acres of the Royal Grant, now called Kingsland, to be laid out next to that of her sister Susannah, and to be by her, and the heirs of her body lawfully begotten, forever quietly and peaceably possessed and enjoyed.

To young Brant *alias* Kaghneghtaga of Canajoharie, I give and bequeath one thousand acres of land in the Royal Grant, now called Kingsland, to be laid out next to and adjoining the before-mentioned land of Anne, daughter of Mary Brant. Also to William, *alias* Tagawirunte, of Canajoharie, one thousand acres of land in said Royal Grant, *alias* Kingsland, adjoining that of Brant, to be by them and the heirs of their body, lawfully begotten, forever quietly and peaceably possessed and enjoyed.

It is also my will and decree, that in case any of the before-mentioned eight children of mine by Mary Brant should die without issue, their share or shares, as well of my personal as real estate, be equally divided amongst the survivors of them by their guardians.

To my prudent and faithful housekeeper, Mary Brant, mother of the before-mentioned eight children, I will and bequeath the lot No. one, being part of the Royal Grant now called Kingsland, and is opposite to the land whereon Honnicol Herkimer now lives, which she is to enjoy peaceably during her natural life; after which it is to be possessed by her son Peter, and his heirs forever; I also give and bequeath to my said housekeeper one negro wench named Jenny, the sister of Juba; also the sum of two hundred pounds, current money of New York, to be paid to her by my executors within three months after my decease; I also devise and bequeath to Mary McGrah, daughter of Christopher McGrah, of the Mohawk country, two hundred acres of land in the patent of Adageghteinge, now called Charlotte River, to be by her and her heirs forever peaceably possessed and enjoyed.

I give and bequeath to my brothers, John and Warren Johnson, to my sisters Dease, Sterling, Plunkent, and Fitzsimons, the following tracts of land, which I would have sold by my executors to the best advantage, and moneys arising therefrom to be equally divided among them and their heirs, to wit: whatever part of the patent called Byrne's at Schoharie, may remain unsold at my decease; also my fourth part of another patent at Schoharie called Lawyer & Zimmer's patent; also that of Adageghteinge or Charlotte River; and lastly, the five thousand acres which I have in Glen and Vrooman's patent; also the thirteen thousand acres which I have in the patent called Peter Servis near General Gage's or whatever part of the aforesaid tracts may be unsold at the time of my decease; this, (from the many losses which I have sustained, and the several sums expended by me during the war which were never paid), is all I can possibly do for them without injuring others, which my honor and conscience will not admit of. As his present Majesty, George the third, was graciously pleased as a mark of his favor and regard, to give me a patent under the great seal for the tract of land now called Kingsland, and that without quit rent, except a trifling acknowledgment to be paid yearly, it is my will and desire that no part of it be ever sold by those to whom I have devised it, as that would be acting contrary to my intentions and determined resolution.

I devise and bequeath to my much esteemed nephew Doctor John Dease the sum of five hundred pounds current money of New York, to be paid to him within six months after my decease by my executors out of such moneys as I may have in this country at that time, or by my son, Sir John, for which he, my said son Sir John Johnson, shall have and forever enjoy that lot of land in Sacandaga patent whereon Martin Laffler and two more tenants now live, viz: No. eighty-four, containing two hundred and fifty acres. I also devise and bequeath unto my said nephew, John Dease, Esq., two thousand acres of land lying near to South Bay, or Lake Champlain, which tract was purchased by me of Lt. Augustine Prevost, and which was formerly the location of Ensign or Lt. Gorvel, with all the advantages thereunto belonging; or should he, my said nephew, prefer or rather choose to have the value of it in money, in that case it is my will and desire that my executors dispose of said land to the best

Old Fireplace, Guy Park.

Will of Sir William Johnson

advantage and pay the amount of it to my said nephew.

To my faithful friend, Robert Adams, Esq., of Johnstown, the dwelling house, other buildings, and the lot and one acre whereon he now lives, the Potash laboratory, and one acre of land with it; also the farm which he holds by deed from me, all free from rent during his natural life, except the quit rent.

To Mr. William Byrne, of Kingsborough, I give the lot of land whereon he now lives and improvements; also that part of the stock of cattle which was mine, free of rent or demand, as long as he lives, the quit rent excepted.

I also will and bequeath to Mr. Patrick Daly, now living with me, for whom I have a particular regard, the sum of one hundred pounds current money of New York, to be paid unto him within three months after my decease, by my executors. It is also my will and desire that all the white servants I may have at the time of my death be made free and receive from my son ten pounds each.

I also devise and bequeath unto my much esteemed friend and old acquaintance, Joseph Chew, Esq., now of Kingsborough, in the county of Tryon, during his natural life, fifty acres of land, which I purchased from Matthias Link, with all the buildings and other improvements thereon belonging; and after his decease, to his son William, my god-child, and to his heirs forever. In case of the death of my said god-son William without issue, then to be possessed and enjoyed by Joseph Chew, junr., elder brother of my said god-son William, and his heirs forever. I also devise and bequeath unto the said Joseph Chew, Esq., two hundred acres of land in the patent called Preston's, now Mayfield, to be laid out in one piece next to the lots already laid out by John Collins, Esq., for the township; the same two hundred acres with all the appurtenances thereto belonging, to be by him, the said Joseph Chew and his heirs, forever peaceably and quietly possessed and enjoyed.

It is also my will and desire, that in case my son Sir John Johnson should (which God avert) die without issue, the following disposition be made of the personal and real estate, which is by the foregoing part of this will bequeathed to him, to wit: all the lands of Kingsborough, containing about fifty thousand acres, the few lots excepted which I have otherwise disposed of, to be by my grandson William Claus, and the heirs of his body, quietly and peaceably possessed and enjoyed; also twenty thousand acres of the Royal Grant, now called Kingsland, which is never to be sold or alienated from my family.

It is likewise my will and desire, that in the above case, viz., of my son's death without issue, that the lands, house, &c., at Fort Johnson, and a small tract on the opposite side of the Mohawk River, called Babington's, together with twenty thousand acres of the Royal Grant, now called Kingsland, be possessed and enjoyed by the first male heir which my daughter Mary Johnson may have by Guy Johnson, and by his heirs lawfully begotten forever; and in case of her having no male heir to possess it, then it is my will that the before-mentioned lands be equally divided between her daughters and their heirs, in consideration of which my two sons-in-law, Daniel Claus and Guy Johnson, shall (within a year) pay unto my executors and trustees for the use of my children by Mary Brant, my housekeeper, the sum of eight hundred pounds current money of New York: that is to say, Colonel Daniel Claus shall pay the sum of five hundred pounds, and Colonel Guy Johnson the sum of three hundred pounds, which sums are to be (as well as the rest devised and bequeathed to them), put out to interest for their support and emolument until they come of age or marry, when equal division is to be made by their guardians or trustees. All the remainder of my son's estate, except what remains of his share in the Royal Grant *alias* Kingsland, shall be sold by my executors to the best advantage, and the moneys arising from the sale thereof to be equally divided between my brothers and sisters as before named, the remainder of his share in Kingsland to be equally divided between his two sisters' children, who are never to dispose of it.

Lastly, I do hereby make, constitute and appoint my beloved son Sir John Johnson, Kt., my two sons-in-law. Daniel Claus and Guy Johnson, Esqs., my two brothers John and Warren Johnson, Esqs., Daniel Campbell, of Schenectady,

West Room, Old Fort Johnson.

Will of Sir William Johnson

John Butler, Nelles Fonda, Captain James Stevenson, of Albany, Robert Adams, Samuel Stringer of Albany, Doctor John Dease, Henry Frey and Joseph Chew, Esqs., or any six of them, executors of this, my last Will and testament. And it is also my will and desire that John Dease, Nelles Fonda, John Butler, James Stevenson, Henry Frey and Joseph Chew, Esqs., be and act as guardians and trustees of my beforementioned eight children by Mary Brant, my present housekeeper, in full confidence that from the close connection of the former, and the long uninterrupted friendship subsisting between me and the latter, they will strictly act as brothers, and inviolably observe and execute this my last charge to them; the strong dependence on, and expectation of which unburthens my mind, allays my cares, and makes a change the less alarming. And as I would willingly, in some measure, (although trifling); testify my regard and friendship for the above mentioned gentlemen, I must request their acceptance of three hundred pounds currency to purchase rings as a memento for their once sincere friend, which sum is to be immediately paid to them by my son, Sir John Johnson. And I do hereby revoke, disannul and make void all former wills, bequests and legacies by me heretofore at any time made, bequeathed or given; and I do hereby make and declare this only to be my last will and testament. In witness whereof I have (with a perfect mind and memory), hereunto set my hand and seal this 27th day of January, 1774, one thousand seven hundred and seventy-four, and my name at the bottom of each page, being thirteen.

W. JOHNSON, (L. S.)

Signed, sealed, published, and declared by the testator as and for his last will and testament, in the presence of us, who, by the desire and in the presence of the said testator and of each other, have hereunto subscribed our names.

WILLIAM ADAMS,
GILBERT TICE,
MOSES IBBIT,
SAMUEL SUTTON.

Tryon Co., *ss*.

Be it remembered that on the twenty-fifth day of July, one thousand seven hundred and seventy-four, personally came and appeared before me, Bryan Lefferty, Surrogate of the said county, Sir John Johnson, Bart., Guy Johnson, Daniel Claus, John Dease, John Butler, Robert Adams and Joseph Chew, executors of the within written will of Sir William Johnson, Bart., and were duly sworn to the true execution and performance of the said will, by severally taking the oath of an executor as by law appointed before me,

BRYAN LEFFERTY,
Surrogate.

Tryon Co., *ss*.

Be it also remembered that on the twenty-fifth day of July, one thousand seven hundred and seventy-four, William Adams, Gilbert Tice, Moses Ibbit, and Samuel Sutton, all of Johnstown and county aforesaid, being duly sworn on their oaths, declared: That they and each of them did see Sir William Johnson, Bart., sign and seal the within written instrument, purporting to be the will of the said Sir William Johnson, bearing date the twenty-seventh day of January, one thousand seven hundred and seventy-four, and heard him publish and declare the same as and for his last will and testament. That at the time thereof he, the said Sir William Johnson, was of sound, disposing mind and memory, to the best of the knowledge and belief of them the deponents. And that their names, subscribed to the said will, are of their respective proper hand-writing, which they subscribed as witnesses to the said will in the testator's presence.

BRYAN LEFFERTY,
Surrogate.

A Corner of Old Guy Park.

CHAPTER XIII

GENEALOGY OF THE JOHNSON FAMILY

I. WILLIAM JOHNSON, Esq. [afterwards knight and baronet], was born at Smith Town, County Meath, Ireland, and subsequently adopted by his maternal uncle, Admiral Sir Peter Warren, K. B., capturer of Louisburg, &c., and went out with him to North America, where he rose to the rank of colonel in the British army, Major-General of the provincial forces and [or] of the militia, 16th April, 1783, and distinguished himself as a military commander during the French [American] War [1754–63], and as a negotiator with Indian tribes. He was created a baronet 27th Nov., 1755. In 1756 he received his commission as "Colonel, Agent and Sole Superintendent of all the affairs of the Six Nations and other Northern Indians," "with no subordination but to Loudon [London?]." He died 11th July, 1774, of chronic malignant dysentery, aged 59, at his seat, Johnson Hall, Tryon County, New York, leaving by Catherine Wisenberg [Weissenberg?], his wife:

   I. JOHN, his heir.
   II. Anne, married to Col. Daniel Claus, of North America, and died about 1798.
   III. Mary, married to Col. Guy Johnson, and had two daughters: 1. Mary, wife of Field Marshal Lord Clyde, queller of the East India mutiny, originally Sir Colin Campbell, and mother of Gen. Sir Guy Campbell; 2. Julia.

The son and heir of Sir William Johnson, Bart.:

II. Sir JOHN JOHNSON, of Johnson Hall, Tryon (afterwards Fulton) County, N. Y., finally of Mount Johnson, Montreal; colonel of regiment of horse in the northern district of New

York, in 1773; Major-General of the militia belonging to the same portion of the province after the decease of his father; lieut.-col. commanding the loyal or provincial "King's Royal Regiment of New York," otherwise "The Queen's Loyal New Yorkers" or "Johnson's regiment of Queen's Royal Greens"; colonel, B. A., 21st October, 1782; Brigadier-General of the provincial troops, &c., 14th March, 1782; superintendent-general and inspector-general of the Six Nations of Indians and their confederates, of all the Indians inhabiting the province of Quebec and the frontier, 16th September, 1791 [a copy of Sir John's commission]; colonel-in-chief of the six battalions of the militia of the eastern townships of Lower Canada. He was knighted at St. James's, London, 22d Nov., 1765. [On the death of his father, Sir William [I.], Sir John positively refused to accept the succession to the former's dignities and offices in connection with the Indians, and they were conferred upon his cousin, Guy Johnson, who exercised them throughout the Revolutionary War, and thus Sir John and Col. Guy have often been confounded, to the disadvantage of Sir John. Sabine says, "Col. Guy Johnson's intemperate zeal for his royal master caused the first affray in that [Tryon] county."] Sir John married, 30th June, 1773, Mary, daughter of Hon. John Watts, Senior, Esq., sometime President of the King's Council of New York, and by her (who died 7th August, 1815) he had issue:

 I. William, lieut.-col., born 1775; married, in 1802, Susan—an extraordinary beauty—daughter of Stephen de Lancey, Governor of Tobago, and sister of Sir William de Lancey, K. C. B., "Quartermaster-General of Wellington's army," killed at Waterloo; and died 1812, leaving by her [who married, secondly, 1815, General Sir Hudson Lowe, K. C. B., and died 1832] three daughters:

  1. Charlotte, married, in 1820, Alexander Count Balmain, Russian commissioner at St. Helena, and died in 1824.
  2. Mary, died unmarried in 1814.
  3. Susan, died unmarried in 1828.

 II. Adam Gordon, IIId baronet.

The Johnson Family

III. James Stephen, captain 28th regiment, killed at Badajoz, born in 1785.
IV. Robert Thomas, drowned in Canada in 1812.
V. Warren, major 68th regiment, died 1813.
VI. John, of Point Oliver, Montreal, col. commanding 6th battalion of militia, born 8th August, 1782; married 10th February, 1825, Mary Diana, daughter of Richard Dillon, Esq., of Montreal, and died 23d June, 1841, leaving issue:
  1. William George, successor to his uncle, and present (in 1882) baronet.
  2. Charles, captain Madras Artillery, born 4th February, 1833.
  3. James Stephen, lieut. 14th foot, born 5th March, 1836; killed at Barbadoes.
  4. Archibald Kennedy, born 20th June, 1839.
  1. Maria Diana.
  2. Anne Margaret.
  3. Eliza Theresa.
  4. Mary Anne.
VII. Charles Christopher, of Argenteuil, Canada East, born 29th October, 1798: lieut.-col. in the army; knight of the second class of the Persian Order of the Lion and Sun; married, 1818, Susan, eldest daughter of Admiral Sir Edward Griffiths, of Northbrook House, Hants [Hampshire] [who took the surname of Colpoys], and died 30th September, 1854, leaving:
  1. William, an officer in 20th regiment, born 28th May, 1821, deceased.
  2. John Ormsby, captain Royal Navy; born 11th August, 1822.
  3. Charles Turquand, born 17th June, 1825, deceased.
  4. Edward Colpoys, born 11th August, 1855, an officer in the army.
  1. Maria Bowes, married, 18th June, 1867, Rev. Wm. Bell Christian, of Ewanrigg Hall, Cumberland, and Milntown, Isle of Man.

2. Mary Anne Susan.

VIII. Archibald Kennedy, born in 1792; married, 13th September, 1818, Maria Johnson, daughter of Patrick Langan, Esq., of Montreal, died 8th October, 1866.
   1. Anne, married to Col. Edward Macdonnell, deputy quartermaster-general to the forces in Canada, who died in 1812.
   2. Catherine Maria, one of the loveliest, wisest, and best of women, married in 1805 to Major-General Barnard Foord Bowes, an officer of unusual ability and intrepidity, who fell in the attack upon the forts at Salamanca, 23d June, 1812. [See Harper's *Alison*, III., 476 (2), and note, and other authorities on the War in Spain]. She died at Anglesey, near Gosport, England, in 1850.
   3. Marianne, died 1st January, 1868.

Sir John died 4th January, 1830, and was succeeded by his eldest surviving son—

III. Sir ADAM GORDON JOHNSON, lieut.-col., of the 6th battalion of militia, born 6th May, 1781; who died unmarried 21st May, 1843, and was succeeded by his nephew, William George, the present (1882) baronet.

IV. Sir WILLIAM GORDON JOHNSON, of Twickenham, County of Middlesex, England, was graduated at Woolwich, and for the best portion of his life held a commission in the British army as captain of artillery, and acted in the discharge of various staff duties, at different posts, and once upon the island of St. Helena; born 19th December, 1830; succeeded as IV. baronet at the decease of his uncle, in May, 1843.

ARMS.—Argent, two lions counter-rampant, supporting a dexter hand, gules; in chief, three estoilles of the last, and in bas, a salmon naiant in water, proper.

CREST.—An arm, gules, encircled with a ducal crown, *or*, the hand grasping a sword, proper, poniard and hilt, *or*.

MOTTO:—"*Nec aspera terrent.*" "*Difficulties do not stop (or deter) or dismay.*" "Boldness wins."

CHAPTER XIV

GIFT OF FORT JOHNSON—MAJOR-GENERAL J. WATTS DE PEYSTER

THIS chapter, in the natural sequence of events, appears late in the book, although in the matter of importance it deserves to appear at the beginning.

The directors of the Montgomery County Historical Society, situated at Amsterdam, N. Y., have long desired to possess the first baronial mansion of Sir William Johnson, known since 1755 as Fort Johnson.

This old structure is situated on the Mohawk River about three miles from the city of Amsterdam, N. Y., and within two hundred feet of the New York Central Railroad on the north, and is plainly visible to tourists from the windows of the cars.

Between 1859 and 1905 the property belonged to and was the home of the family of Ethan Akin, who died in 1897. In 1905 this property was sold, in order to settle the estate. In order to save the old building from being put to improper use the Historical Society above mentioned obtained an option on the property for sixty days by making a cash payment of five hundred dollars. Before the sixty days had elapsed, Major-General J. Watts de Peyster of "Rose Hill," Tivoli. N. Y., became interested in the preservation of the old mansion for family reasons, and offered to purchase Fort Johnson (price $5900) and deed it to the society, provided the said society would assume to care for and maintain the same and to install a suitable bronze tablet in the interior. The society having agreed to these provisions, the General proceeded to carry out his part of the contract and the transfer of the property was made on November 9, 1905.

Suitable resolutions were engrossed and sent to the General and in various other ways the people of the city of Amsterdam have expressed their appreciation of his generous gift.

Below will be found a short sketch of Major-General de Peyster and some of his notable ancestors:

John Watts de Peyster, brevet major-general, by special act of New York State Legislature, for "meritorious services rendered to the National Guard and to the United States, prior to and during the Rebellion." On his father's side he can trace back his descent under most favorable circumstances for six hundred years in Flanders, especially in Ghent, where his people continually held offices which to hold was peculiarly the right of those of noble or aristocratic lineage. As far back as the thirteenth century they suffered on account of their acceptance of Protestant or Reformed doctrines and were faithful, even to the death, to their opinions. They were termed Huguenots, although it is generally considered the term is only applicable to Frenchmen, but the de Peysters belonged to districts which are now French territory, constituting the "Nord" and the "Pas de Calais." On his mother's side, Watts, the record is equally striking and honorable. The family residence was a very imposing building 60 feet square, besides the offices, three stories high, originally just outside but latterly within the city limits of Edinburgh. The site was remarkable as affording exquisite views to the northwest, west and southwest. This Watts residence—still standing within half a century—was torn down and the site

J. Watts de Peyster,
From a steel engraving.

and domain became the property of the Caledonian Railroad. John Watt, whose daughter married Sir Walter Riddel, whose baronetcy dated back to the reign of King David I. (twelfth century), was a very remarkable city functionary and held the office of dean of the guilds, or deacon-convener then a most important position of authority and influence. When his King, James VI. of Scotland, was besieged in the old Tolbooth and the lives of himself and his court were threatened by a vicious mob incited by the Calvinist clergy, John Watt called his guilds to arms and rescued the King, and thereby saved his native city from the punishment of military execution. This brave gentleman was afterwards assassinated in revenge for his loyalty, instigated by the same Calvinist ministers and party, and his murderer escaped through their influence. His grandson Robert Watt emigrated to New York and for some unknown reason added an *s* to the name and thus became Watts, and at the same time the Nichols family, his wife's, dropped the *s* and became Nichol.

The subject of this sketch is remarkable for the variety of distinguishing features which have been shown by his successful powers of practical and elegant designs, powers of research and composition in painting and sculpture and architecture, wherein, as professionals admitted, if they had listened to him success would have rewarded them for their attention, and failing to do so, they came short of success. The first was displayed in the membership diploma (the handsomest in the States) of the Holland Society, for which he received a most flattering vote of thanks or resolution; and this power is also shown in his practical plans of public buildings which he has erected, *i.e.*, his church as a memorial of his two daughters, his fireman's hall in memory of his two eldest sons, both in the village of Madalin, and his Watts de Peyster Home for Invalid Children in the township of Unionvale.

The first public building in which he was interested was the completion of an Episcopal church at Natchitoches, which was the first Protestant place of worship in that district. When a regiment from Dutchess County, N. Y., occupied that city during the Red River expedition the men climbed into the belfry, and were surprised at finding a bell bearing a dedicatory inscription and the name of the donor, a fellow-countryman. During the slaveholders' rebellion the edifice was neglected so it had to be entirely restored, which was done in 1900 at the expense of General de Peyster, by whom it was originally completed. The General seems to have survived almost every one with whom he was intimate of his associates of boyhood days and his school companions, and, when he applied to the first rector of the Maria de Peyster Memorial Church at Natchitoches for interesting particulars in regard thereto, the answer was the Rev. Thomas Scott Bacon had just died.

A short time since General de Peyster conveyed Rose Hill—named after his ancestral home in Scotland, above alluded to—his home near Tivoli station, to the Leake and Watts Orphan House at Yonkers, founded and endowed by his maternal grandfather, John Watts, reserving for himself the use of the property for life. He has just presented Fort Johnson, a historic family property, at Akin, N. Y., to the Montgomery County Historical Society. Among other benefactions of the General are: A home for consumptives in Unionvale, Dutchess County, the first of the kind so devoted, which was burned; St. Paul's Training School for Boys, at Unionvale; established and endowed the Watts de Peyster Industrial Home and School for Girls, with its buildings and extensive grounds, at Madalin. To the city of Kearney, Neb., General de Peyster presented a bronze bust of his cousin Major-General Philip Kearney. He erected a chapel at Nebraska City as a memorial of his dead soldier sons—afterwards pulled down and the Watts de Peyster tablets transferred to a church in Kearney. At Altoona, Pa., he finished a church and built a memorial parish school and parsonage in memory of his daughter, Maria Beata. For Franklin and Marshall College, Lancaster, Pa., he erected and equipped a very fine library building, and to the Leake and Watts Orphan House, at Yonkers, N. Y., he gave funds for an annex and added a donation of property valued at $200,000. To the State capitols of New York, Pennsylvania and New Jersey

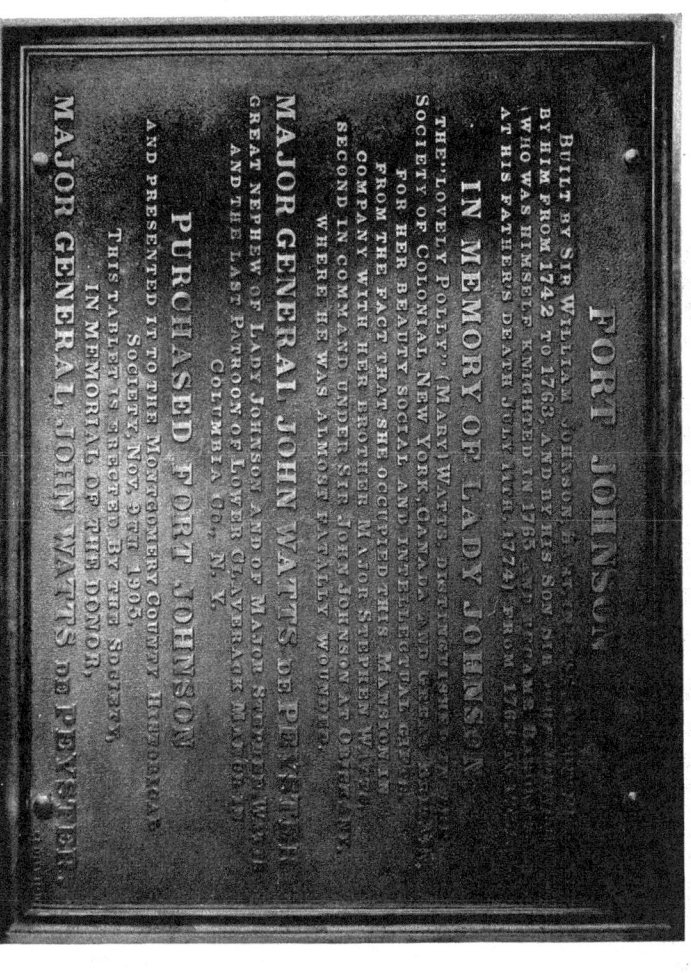

Memorial Tablet Erected in Honor of Major General John Watts de Peyster.

Hon. Stephen Sanford.

General de Peyster

General de Peyster has presented bronzes and oil paintings of various distinguished relatives. He has given a most valuable and in some respects inestimable collection on Napoleon and on other subjects, comprising objects of art, bronzes, pictures, etc., to the library of the Smithsonian Institution, to which he is still adding.

In the city of New York are several statues of heroic size in commemoration of historic members of his family. In Trinity churchyard stands a bronze statue of the General's grandfather, the Hon. John Watts, Jr., the last Royal recorder of New York; in the Bowling Green is a bronze statue of his famous ancestor Colonel Abraham de Peyster, a public-spirited citizen of the early period of Manhattan's history. Opposite this statue General de Peyster was himself born, in the old Watts residence at No. 3 Broadway, 9th March, 1821. No. 1 Broadway was built by his great-uncle the Earl of Cassilis.

General de Peyster is a life member of the Royal Historical Society of Great Britain, honorary fellow of the Society of Science, Letters and Arts of London, and member of the Maatschappij der Nederlandsche Letterkunde of Leyden, Holland, etc., etc. He is of the seventh generation resident of the first ward, city of New Amsterdam, afterward New York, and the sixth born therein in the course of two centuries and a half, and his family's connection with Dutchess County has extended over seven generations.

The General was sent to Europe in 1851 as military agent of the State of New York. One of the results of that commission was the establishment of a paid fire department with steam fire engines and the organization of the present municipal police of New York city. In proof the General holds letters or certificates and testimonials from the highest officials.

At the beginning of the Civil War General de Peyster offered his services as Brigadier-General, with three picked regiments, to President Lincoln. Conditions prevented the acceptance of the offer, but two of his sons served with credit throughout the struggle, and all three of his sons were brevetted colonel for services rendered before they came of age. He repeated his offer of troops, but it was again refused. He was reviled by his neighbors for suggesting the use of negroes as soldiers in the Civil War, and Southerners upbraided him for defending John Brown, but he upheld his opinions. He saved the Italian soldier Siro Pesci, a follower of Mazzini, from condemnation to a living death in the salt mines of Sardinia and smuggled him from Italy into France, and subsequently to Switzerland.

Both his maternal and paternal ancestors suffered greatly in body, person and property for their loyalty, "faithful even unto death," to their kings and religious beliefs in Europe and America, and it was only when the slaveholders' rebellion occurred that they had the good fortune of finding themselves on the winning side. It was religious persecution that drove the de Peysters of Flanders to seek refuge in England and Holland, and from the latter country the General's g.-g.-g.-g.-grandfather emigrated to the New Netherlands, where he immediately exerted influence in city offices; and his great-grandson, whose statue adorns the Bowling Green, opposite the new custom-house, on the spot where he presided as receiver-general of the port in 1705, held in the course of his long life every possible office, even that of acting governor under the Crown, in his native city.

MONTGOMERY COUNTY HISTORICAL SOCIETY—RICHMOND COLLECTION—HON. STEPHEN SANFORD—ENDOWMENT.

On the opposite page will be seen an illustration of a portion of the museum of the Montgomery County Historical Society. As Old Fort Johnson is destined, in the near future, to be the home of this museum, it seems proper that a description of the collection of aboriginal relics which comprise the major part of this museum should appear in these pages.

Richmond Collection

As a rule historical societies are not blessed with large bank accounts, and the above society is no exception to the general rule, the highest ambition of its directors having been to so conduct its affairs as to keep it alive from year to year, doing what little good might come in its way by marking historic sites and preserving records, with an occasional social function during each fiscal year.

At a little village a score of miles away from the city of Amsterdam, bearing the Indian name of Canajoharie, lived Mr. A. G. Richmond, an enthusiastic antiquarian who from boyhood had been interested in locating Indian sites and the collection of aboriginal relics. As his collection grew, through research and by purchase, his knowledge of the uses of the strange stone implements that he had obtained grew also, until at the maturity of his manhood he became an authority on Indian sites both historic and prehistoric, and also became noted as being the possessor of the largest and finest collection of Indian articles of warfare and the chase, and various domestic utensils of the Amerinds, to be found in the Mohawk Valley.

Unfortunately Mr. Richmond died, in the full vigor of his manhood, mourned by many loving friends, and regretted by his colaborers in this fascinating field of research. Fortunately, however, for antiquarians he had prepared, in manuscript, a valuable catalogue of the twenty-two thousand articles comprised in his collection, with most complete details of the uses of these articles, the place where found, and other information valuable to students in this branch of historic research.

Many looked with longing eyes and coveted the possession of these rare articles, but none more eagerly than the president of this association, J. H. Hanson. I know not what trick of alchemy, what persuasive power, what nimbleness of tongue, was used, but suddenly, and as unexpectedly as the glare of the lightning flash from a cloudless sky, it was announced that gold had been given to purchase the coveted Richmond collection.

A man whom all delight to honor, a gentleman whom it is a pleasure to meet, a scholar with mind stored with a rare fund of information and a delightful manner of imparting the same, a man with a generous and beneficent heart and well-filled coffers, Hon. Stephen Sanford, had again given of his wealth to assist a struggling society.

More surely than "storied urn or animated bust" will his many acts of beneficence perpetuate his name to generations yet unborn, a name inseparably connected with the history and prosperity of the city of Amsterdam. Other evidences of his interest in history and historic sites and kindness to the society of which he is an honorary member are his material assistance in the renovation of Old Fort Johnson, and in publishing that valuable book entitled *Minutes of the Committee of Safety of Tryon County*. But the crowning act is the endowing of this historic building with a sufficient sum to perpetuate it and care for it until its time-worn timbers cease to exist and its stone walls crumble to dust.

The total amount given the society up to date by Mr. Sanford is $21,600, as follows:

Statue of Sir William Johnson, Bart., Johnstown, N. Y.

Endowment	$15,000
Richmond Collection	5,000
To publish book	1,000
Renovation of Fort Johnson	600
	$21,600

CHAPTER XV

LAND GRANTS: ROYAL, KINGSBOROUGH, SACANDAGA—
JOHNSON HALL

THE theme of this book being "Old Fort Johnson," it was my intention to confine myself to the history of the old building on the Mohawk River; but there have been so many mistakes made by early writers, and such a confusion in the minds of many in regard to the location of the two homes of Sir William Johnson, that it seems necessary to give more than a cursory allusion to the second baronial mansion of Sir William, located at Johnstown and known as Johnson Hall. The Tryon map of 1779 shows large tracts of land that belonged to his estate situated west, north and south of Fort Johnson, the most notable being the Kingsland patent of forty thousand acres located between East and West Canada creeks. It is said that the tract of land between the creeks mentioned in the patent really contained ninety-three thousand acres instead of forty thousand as mentioned in the Kingsland or Royal grant.

It is known that the Baronet's possessions in the vicinity of Fort Johnson on the Mohawk were somewhat limited on account of earlier grants of land issued to other parties, the Caughnawaga, Hansen, and Butler grants crowding him on the west and

Land Grants

the Kayaderosseros patent on the east. In fact the only land he owned on the north bank of the Mohawk he bought at second hand, the Guy Park square mile having been originally granted (Dec. 12, 1727) to Henry Hoofe and known as the Hoofe patent, and the balance of his estate surrounding Fort Johnson was granted to Wilson and Abeel February 22, 1706, and comprised about two thousand acres of land, more or less. John Abeel, one of the patentees, was the father of the celebrated half-breed Corn-Planter, whose mother is said to have been a daughter of a Seneca chief.

John Abeel is spoken of in the *Colonial Documents* as an Albany trader. He seems to have traded principally with the Senecas, exchanging rum, and other commodities coveted by the Indians, for peltries. That he was a rover, a *coureur du bois*, seems to be true, but tiring of his roving life he married a white woman named Mary Knouts, settled on land about a mile west of Fort Plain, and became a farmer. He spent the remainder of his days on this farm. Simms tells a story which he terms "Captivity of John Abeel":

During the invasion of the Canajoharie settlement, as it was then called, in August, 1780, when John Abeel was about 56 years old, he was captured by a party of Brant's Indians and taken to the flats between his house and the Mohawk River. It is believed that Corn-Planter, who was with Brant, did not know of his father's captivity under several hours.

During the afternoon Abeel's captors came up with another party of Indians, whom Abeel addressed in their own language, which he spoke fluently, inquiring what they meant to do with him. This led to the inquiry where he had learned the Indian language, and also his name. These facts being made known in camp, Abeel was at once confronted by a chief of commanding figure and appearance, who addressing him said: "You, I understand, are John Abeel, once a trader among the Senecas. You are my father! My name is also John Abeel or Gy-ant-wa-chia, the Corn-Planter. I am a warrior and have taken many scalps. You are now my prisoner, but you are safe from all harm! Go with me to my home in the Senecas' country and you shall be kindly cared for. My strong arm shall provide you with corn and venison. There my mother awaits you. But if you prefer to go back among your paleface friends, you shall be allowed to do so, and I will send an escort of trusty Senecas to conduct you back to Fort Plain." The parent chose to return, and early in the evening an escort of Seneca braves left him near the fort. His house had been destroyed and was not rebuilt until the close of the war.

A few years afterwards Abeel developed insanity and became incompetent to manage his farm, but at first did not develop any violent mania. Somewhat later he had some words with one of his negro slaves, and, becoming violently angry, went into his house, obtained a gun and, returning to the field, shot the negro through the head, killing him instantly.

An attempt was made by the neighbors to arrest him, but being threatened with the gun they desisted. He was, however, subsequently arrested, but it was decided that, "as he was insane and that the negro was his own property, and he amenable to no one for his value, he should be confined."

A room was prepared in his own house and he was chained to the floor, where at times he would make night hideous by clanking his chains and executing a war dance. Some years later, in his old age, he became harmless and was allowed to wander about

Johnson Hall, Johnstown, N. Y.

Land Grants

his farm, and finally met his death by being gored by a vicious bull.

The Kingsborough patent was granted to Arent Stevens *and others* on June 23, 1753, and comprised twenty thousand acres, while the Sacandaga patent of twenty-eight thousand was granted to Lendert Gansevoort *and others* December 2, 1741.

During the early years of the settlement of the colony of New York, grants of prodigious size were obtained by single individuals or small companies, but the attempted steal of the immense tract of land comprised in the notorious Kayaderosseros patent aroused Indians and white settlers alike, and a law was passed prohibiting the transfer of more than a thousand acres to one person. This, however, did not prevent an individual from obtaining large tracts of land by forming companies of, say, the purchaser or purchasers and as many dummies or paper men as there were *thousands* of acres in the tract of land desired.

That the Kingsborough and Sacandaga patents were obtained in this way there is no doubt, and that these tracts ultimately became the property of William Johnson is a well-known fact.

Here was room to expand, here was an opportunity to carry out the scheme of his heart since he had been created baronet—the establishment of a barony with manor house and numerous tenantry.

Already farms had been taken up on the Sacandaga patent, and probably a nucleus of a settlement established before the building of Johnson Hall in 1762–1763, as a rude church was erected and a graveyard started (?) as early as 1760. This seems to have been a rude affair, constructed of wood, with large door on one side as was usual in all of the wooden churches of that period that Sir William was instrumental in building. It is said that this old wood structure, being inadequate in size for the growing hamlet, was torn down in 1771 and the foundation of a stone church begun on the southwest corner of the lot. After the walls were raised several feet the plan was changed and a new site selected, being the lot on which St. John's church now stands. In 1836 this structure was burned and was replaced by the present building, although the position on the lot was changed at right angles with the old church, which ran north and south, with an entrance on Church Street, whereas St. John's of to-day stands east and west with entrance on North Market Street.

Johnson Hall was built of wood, and as originally constructed bore a striking resemblance to Mount or Fort Johnson on the Mohawk in everything except the material used, Mount Johnson being constructed of stone, while Johnson Hall was built of wood, the clapboards being arranged to simulate stone blocks with bevelled edges.

There was the same wide hall and open staircase leading to an attic; each story was divided into four rooms, two large square and two long narrow rooms, and the use of panelled walls and wainscoting although not to as great extent as at Fort Johnson. The site of each building was bordered on the east by a creek and in each case the buildings were located low on a wide expanse of meadow or flat lands.

Land Grants

Each building had its kitchen and servants' quarters outside, built of stone, and in each case the lawn in front was dotted with the locust and the lilac. So little taste or originality was displayed in Johnson Hall that it would seem as though it were a temporary structure, one to be replaced by a mansion commensurate with his title and his enormous wealth. At the present time the building has been so changed from its original plain design, so improved, when looked at from the standpoint of the twentieth century, so marred and disfigured, from the colonial point of view, that it cannot be recognized from the cuts that were made before changes were made.

How often the march of time and the requirements of wealth and trade make it necessary to change the appearance or to efface from the face of the earth all track, trace or remembrance of old buildings that become dear to memory as they grow old and fall into decay. The memories are often lasting to the surviving generation that, perhaps, were born and reared within its walls. Such persons will lend an attentive ear to matters pertaining to an old edifice and be in sympathy with efforts made to perpetuate the memory in records of history. Others are somewhat indifferent and are willing to leave the task to some one else. We go across the seas to see ancient castles and cathedrals and look with wonder at their time-worn walls and records, and return to look on with indifference when some old landmark in our own country is ruthlessly destroyed to make room for a structure more to the taste of young America.

Johnson Hall in its present state is an attractive mansion, both the exterior and interior showing evidence of the wealth and refinement of the present owners, but to an antiquary, to a historian, or rather one interested in all the history there is to the valley of the Mohawk and the adjacent country, there is a feeling of disappointment and regret that this building should have been modernized by the addition of piazzas, bay windows, cupola, and sundry changes in the decorations of the interior.

It is surprising, in view of the manifold points of historic interest existing in the vicinity of Johnson Hall, that the citizens of Johnstown have not manifested greater zeal in the early history of this pioneer village with all of its associations connected with the mature life of Sir William Johnson. I presume that it is owing, probably, to the traditions that have survived "the times that tried men's souls," when the passions of men were aroused in that cruel fratricidal warfare when families, even, were divided into Tories and patriots, and where, as at Oriskany, brothers and neighbors fought and met death with knives buried in each other's bodies or rigid fingers clasped around each other's throats. It is said that the "evil men do lives after them, but the good is often interred with their bones." The feeling of rage against the Johnson family, to whom was attributed all of the horror of Indian warfare, survived for a century, and the silly gossip of that period, recorded in the early books of J. R. Simms and others, has perpetuated senseless scandal which have in a measure injured the character of a truly great man in the very

The Mohawk in the Chilly Grasp of Winter.

Land Grants

place he should be most venerated, the Mohawk Valley.

But a change has come o'er the spirit of their dreams, thanks to two or three vigorous historical societies that in the last two decades have produced great results. In addition to Johnson Hall, Johnstown has many interesting buildings of historic value —the court-house, jail, Drum house, St. John's Episcopal church, all built originally by Sir William, and his grave in St. John's churchyard. All of these have been treated at length in a former volume.

The recent erection of a fine granite statue of Sir William, by the Aldine Society, in the small park at the junction of Hall Avenue and West State Street, shows that the historic sentiment had but slumbered and needed but the enthusiastic, strenuous, and united action of the Aldine Society to awake it to life. It is hoped that the historical societies of Johnstown will not cease their efforts until, either by gift, bequest, or purchase, they become the owners of Johnson Hall and sufficient land surrounding it to constitute a public park.[1]

[1] Since the paragraph was put in print, Johnson Hall has become the property of New York State, which I assume will be guarantee for its perpetual preservation.

CHAPTER XVI

SUMMER RAMBLES—SCHOHARIE CREEK FROM SOURCE TO ITS OVERFLOW—SKELETONS OF ABORIGINES—PHOTOGRAPHING THE FOREST AND LAKE SCENERY—A BOULDER THAT WALKED AWAY—HISTORIC CHARACTERS OF TRIBES HILL

IN the Catskill Mountains, a few miles northwest of the Kaaterskill, and at an elevation of about four thousand feet, one of many springs flows from the mountain side in a tiny rivulet, which soon unites with other small streams and goes bounding and dashing through dark and tangled ravines, sometimes lost to sight in dense vegetation, again visible in foaming cascades. Ever descending, it winds its tortuous course to the north, gathering other streams in its embrace, until these nameless rivulets lose the designation of "kills" and are dignified with the Indian name "Schoharie" Creek. Still turbulent it dashes on through Schoharie County, ever descending, ever widening, unharnessed, except in a primitive way, tapping the Helderbergs, draining the Appalachian foothills, through which it flows until it attains the dignity of a river, and a hundred miles from the source forms a junction with the historic Mohawk, at the prehistoric village of Ti-o-non-de-ro-ga, known, since 1712, as Fort Hunter.

Mound at Fort Hunter where a Number of Indian Skeletons Were Uncovered.

Summer Rambles

During the latter part of the winter of 1903-04 this stream gave renewed evidence of its turbulency by pouring great floods, mingled with ice and snow, into the ice-bound Mohawk, forming a gorge below its mouth, endangering a suspension bridge across the Mohawk at Fort Hunter, flooding the extensive flats at this point, and altering the course of the Mohawk so that a section of the Erie Canal, about a mile long, was practically destroyed.

After the warm weather of spring had cleared the watercourses of the accumulation of water and ice, work was begun to put the Erie again in commission, and a thousand men and hundreds of wagons were soon at work filling in the "break" with earth from the surrounding hills and flats. It may be well to state that this section of New York State was formerly the home of the Mohawks of the Six Nations, and probably for many centuries the home of tribes of the Algonquin Indians.

During the necessary excavations human bones were unearthed, but, except in a few instances, did not seem of any significance to the numerous laborers, until the many bones uncovered attracted the attention of a limited number of persons who were familiar with the early history of this section of New York State.

In the early part of May, however, as many as six skeletons were uncovered, three of which were nearly complete. Around the neck of one were the remains of a necklace of wampum, which was estimated to contain about two thousand beads, which in the scramble that ensued among the Italian workmen were widely distributed or entirely lost, with the exception of about three hundred, that were obtained by Foreman

Martin J. Hartley, who also secured the skeleton. Another collection of bones in a fair state of preservation was secured by N. Burton Alter, of Fort Hunter.

The third skeleton, secured by the writer, was more complete than the others and proved of great value on account of the finding of a portion of an Indian jar of large size in the grave with the bones, being positive evidence that the remains were those of an Indian, and that the place where they were uncovered was an ancient burial place of the Amerinds.

Recently I again visited this spot and obtained photographs of the vicinity. The day, although warm, was one of those "rare days in June" when the air, the sun, the sky, the wooded hills, and the vast extent of flat lands tempted one to explore this enchanting section of the beautiful Mohawk Valley, and to revel in the great wealth of verdure covering hundreds of acres of flat lands extending to the east and to the west. "Peace, peace, perfect peace," pervaded the spot. Nearly a mile away to the west the little village was scarcely visible through the screen of tall elms that intercepted the view, and the only sound heard was the creak of the tiller of a canal boat, and the clang of the bell of a hidden schoolhouse. To the south were wooded hills and north the Mohawk River, while midway the sluggish flow of the Erie Canal shone like a ribbon of burnished silver in the noonday sun. At our feet lay a small lake, half covered with green rushes and bordered with shrubs and low trees covered with the dense foliage of leaves in the luxuriance of full maturity.

Screening the Mohawk from view was an elevation of about twenty feet, and two acres in extent, covered with a grove of large forest trees. A new road through the edge of this grove led to one of the excavations that had been made in repairing the canal. This was the spot where the greatest number of bones were found.

One of the pictures taken was a view of the small lake in close proximity to the knoll. In selecting a point of view for this picture, the Professor wandered up and down the margin of the lake, and at last set his tripod down in front of me near the shore. I was barely conscious of an object in the grass, within a couple of feet from my position, which I had taken to be a good-sized boulder. An exclamation from my friend centred my attention, and the object was seen to heave, and I became aware that my boulder was an immense turtle, whose huge bulk was half concealed in the high grass. "Shall I turn it on its back?" I asked the Professor. "Do you think you can?" was the response. Reaching down I grasped the off side of the shell; out came four great legs armed with sharp claws about an inch in length, while the horrid reptilian head, as large as my wrist, reached for my hand and I dropped the ponderous body, which with an awkward movement sped down the sharp incline and disappeared in the lake in a muddy cloud which marked its course and at the same time concealed its destination. Not till then did I realize that I had had in my grasp a monster turtle that had eluded capture for many months. "It is a fortunate thing for you," said the Professor, "that that wide mouth did not catch your fingers, because, as the old saying has it, 'a turtle never looses its hold until it thunders.'"

Having obtained our quest, but lost the turtle, we turned our steps homeward, which in this case was away from home, in order to reach a bridge and make a visit to Tribes Hill, pleasantly situated on a large plateau about two hundred feet above the Mohawk River.

The earliest record that I can find of Tribes or "Trips" Hill, as it is called on the Tryon map of 1779, is a grant of two thousand acres of land in the town of Mohawk to "Hendrick Hansen and his son Hans" dated 1713. The first settlers are said to have been respectable yeomen, being the family of Nicholas Hansen, who emigrated from Albany about 1725. His son, Frederick, is said to have been the first white child born on the north side of the Mohawk River in this vicinity. Other settlers came in 1728, a New Englander named Bowen, and Victor Putman from Schenectady. With the assistance of Dewitt C. Putman and Pearson's history of the Schenectady patent I am able to trace the genealogy of the Putman family back to Jan Putman, Goor, Holland, born probably in the latter part of the sixteenth century. A story is told which deals with the descendants of the two pioneers:

It is said that conspicuous among the Tories who accompanied Sir John Johnson in his raid in the Mohawk Valley on May 20, 1780, were Henry and William Bowen, who were active in the massacre of their neighbors on that awful night. The most zealous Whig at the "Hill" was Garret Putman, a great-grandson of the original settler, Victor Putman, and captain of a company of rangers. He had rendered himself particularly obnoxious to the British and Tories as a

Great Turtle Pond, Fort Hunter, N. Y.

fearless and zealous patriot. On May 18, 1780, two days before the stealthy attack of Sir John and his Indians and Tories, he was ordered to repair to Fort Hunter; probably for garrison duty, as he took his family with him, and rented his house to two Englishmen named William Gort and James Plateau. Although the sympathies of Gort and Plateau were with the British they had taken no active part in the struggle that was going on, and were therefore unmolested by the patriots.

About midnight on the 20th, a party of marauders were stealthily approaching the dwelling-house of Mr. Putman. The waning moon half disclosed the dusky forms of the painted Indians and the half-disguised Tories, former neighbors of their helpless and unsuspecting victims. The crash of doors and windows as the invaders forced an entrance into their victims' home was made doubly terrifying mingled as it was with the war cry of the savages and the shouts of the whites as they killed and scalped the inmates, supposing them to be Mr. Putman and his son. But the dawn of the day and the vivid glare of burning dwellings and barns revealed the forms of their friends, Gort and Plateau, whom they had mistaken for the Putmans. The same night Henry Hansen was also killed.

Many tales are told of that dreadful night, when the unsuspecting inhabitants of the Hill were aroused from their peaceful slumbers to seek safety in flight from the Indians and the equally cruel Tories (whose fiendish natures had been aroused in this cruel partisan war by the example of the Butlers and Johnsons), or to meet a cruel death by tomahawks and scalping knives in the hands of these ruthless marauders. A story is told of the subsequent part of this raid, which was continued up the valley. Having destroyed the residence of Col. Fisher, who was scalped and left for dead, and his two brothers, John and Herman, killed, they proceeded to the house of Adam Fonda, which was pillaged and destroyed, and Mr. Fonda captured. Before the house was burned one of the Tories stole a large and massive copper tea-kettle, which he filled with butter and hid in the water under a bridge near by, expecting to return that way and get it, but the militia gathering in the rear of Sir John Johnson forced him to return by the way of Johnstown. After the war this kettle was found, and returned to the family of Adam Fonda, and is now in possession of the family of his granddaughter, Mrs. John H. Striker, of Tribes Hill.

It was for the purpose of obtaining a photograph of this interesting relic of the times that tried men's souls that we made our visit to Tribes Hill.

The Jelles Fonda Copper Kettle. A Revolution Relic.

CHAPTER XVII

THE EARLY MOHAWK INDIANS' IDEA OF THE "CREATION"

I AM somewhat at a loss to select a name for the subject of this chapter. I dare not dignify it by the title of a history of the Mohawks, because a true history of that notable people never has been nor ever can be written. It is true that Colden's *Five Nations*, Morgan's *League of the Iroquois*, and Schoolcraft's notes are looked upon as authority on this subject; but Morgan's work is in a great measure legendary, and altogether unsatisfying, and the same may be said of Colden and Schoolcraft, although the little that Colden has to say about the Mohawks is accepted as authority as far as it goes.

As to the origin of the Mohawks, it will always remain a mystery. Conjecture may or may not approach the truth, but from the fact that they had no written language, no records on stone or parchment from which we can obtain knowledge of their origin or early history, it is evident that our only sources of information are the vague traditions that have been transmitted orally from parent to child or from sachem to sachem.

How unreliable and unsatisfactory these oral traditions are may be noted in what is called the *Iroquoian*

Cosmology as translated by J. N. B. Hewitt, of the Bureau of Ethnology. Mr. Hewitt gives three versions of the "creation," the Onondaga, Mohawk, and the Seneca. They are practically alike, differing only in minor statements. The Onondaga is the longest and the Seneca the shortest version. I will give you, however, a condensed rendering of the Mohawk tradition; it says:

In the sky above were man-beings, both male and female, who dwelt in villages, and in one of the lodges was a man and woman, who were down-fended, that is, they were secluded, and their lodge was surrounded by the down of the cat-tail, which was a sign that no one should approach them, nor were they allowed to leave this precinct. The man became ill, and stated that he would not get well until a dogwood tree standing in his door-yard had been uprooted. So when his people had uprooted the tree he said to his wife, "Do thou spread for me something there beside the place where stood the tree." Thereupon she spread something for him there and he then lay down on what she had spread for him, and he said to his wife: "Here sit thou, beside my body." Now at that time she did sit beside him as he lay there. Then he said to her: "Do thou hang thy legs down into the abyss." For where they had uprooted the tree there came to be a deep hole, which went through the sky, and the earth was upturned about it.

And while he lay there he recovered from his illness and turning on his side he looked into the hole. "After a while he said to his wife, 'Do thou look thither into the hole, to see what things are occurring there in yonder place.' And as she bent her body to look into the hole he took her by the nape of the neck and pushed her, and she fell into the hole and kept falling into the darkness thereof. After a while she passed through and as she looked about her, as she slowly fell, she saw that all about her

The Author Restoring the Great Mohawk Jar.

was blue in color, and soon discovered that what she observed was a vast expanse of water on which floated all kinds of water-fowls in great numbers.

Thereupon Loon looking into the waters and seeing her reflection shouted, "A man-being, a female, is coming up from the depths of the waters." The Bittern answering said, "She is not indeed coming up out of the depths of the water, she is falling from above." Thereupon they held a council to decide what they should do to provide for her welfare.

They finally invited Great Turtle to come. Loon thereupon said to him: "Thou shouldst float thy body above the place where thou art in the depths of the water." And then, as Great Turtle arose to the surface, a large body of ducks of various kinds arose from the face of the water, elevated themselves in a very compact body, and went up to meet her. And on their backs did she alight, and they slowly descended bearing her body on their backs, and on the back of Great Turtle they placed her.

Then Loon said, "Come, you deep divers, dive and bring up earth." Many dived in the water, and Beaver was a long time gone. When his back appeared he was dead, and when they examined his paws they found no earth. Then Otter said, "It is my turn." Whereupon he dived and after a longer time he also came up dead. Neither did he bring up any earth. It was then that Muskrat said, "I also will make the desperate attempt." It was a still longer time that he was under water, but after a while he also floated to the surface dead. In his paws was mud and his mouth was full of mud. And they took this mud and coated the edge of Great

Turtle's shell all around, and other muskrats dived and floated dead, but brought up mud, which was placed on Great Turtle's back. And the female man-being sat on the back of Great Turtle and slept. And when she awoke the earth had increased in size, and she slept again, and when she awoke willows were growing along the edge of the water. And then, also, when she again awoke the carcass of a deer, recently killed, lay there, and a fire was burning, and a sharp stone. And she dressed, cooked, and ate her fill. And after a while a rivulet appeared and rapidly the earth increased to great size, and grass and herbs sprung from the earth and grew to maturity.

And after a while the female man-being gave birth to a girl child, who grew rapidly to maturity and not long after gave birth to two male man-beings, but the daughter died in giving birth to the twins. And the grandmother cut off the head of her dead daughter and hung her body in a high place, and it became the sun, and the head she placed in another place and it became the moon.

And when she examined one of the infants she found his flesh was nothing but flint and there was a sharp comb of flint over the top of his head, but the flesh of the other was in every respect like a man-being.

It seems that these two were antagonistic from their birth, the grandmother clinging to the flint child and driving the other into the wilderness; and in his wanderings he came to the shore of a lake and saw a lodge standing there. Looking in the doorway he saw a man sitting there, who said to him, "Enter thou here." This man was Great Turtle, who gave him bow and arrow and also gave him two ears of corn, one in the milky state which he told him to roast and eat as food, and the other, which was mature, he should use for seed corn.

He also endowed him with preternatural powers. And when he was about to depart he said to the young man, "I am Great Turtle, I am thy parent."

Sapling, which was the name of the young man-being' created animals out of earth, and birds by casting handfuls of earth into the air. He also formed the body of a man and the body of a woman and gave them life and placed them together. Returning shortly after he found them sleeping. Again and again he returned and still they slept. "Thereupon he took a rib from each and substituted the one for the other and replaced each one in the other's body. It was not long before the woman awoke and sat up. At once she touched the breast of the man lying at her side just where Sapling had placed her rib, and, of course, that tickled him. Thereupon he awoke, awoke to life and understanding." As in the Biblical story of Cain and Abel, the two brothers fought and in the end one was slain. But it was the unrighteous one, the one with the flint body, who lost his life.

Nearly three hundred years ago, the Jesuits recorded traditions of the Algonquins and Huron-Iroquois of Canada which were practically the same in their main features as the above. (See *Jesuit Relations*, vol. x, pages 127–129.)

The Montagnais and Adirondacks of Canada, and in fact all the Algonquin nations, seem to have some tradition of the deluge, which, in some way is mixed with the Huron-Iroquois tradition of the creation. In fact it deals with a re-creation of the earth.

They say that one Messou restored the world when it was lost in the waters. Their story of the deluge is practically as follows:

This Messou went a-hunting with lynxes instead of dogs and was warned that it would be dangerous for his lynxes in a certain lake near the place where he was. One day as he was hunting an elk his lynxes gave it chase even into the lake; and when they reached the middle of it, they were submerged in an instant. When Messou arrived there and sought his lynxes, who were indeed his brothers, a bird told him that it had seen them in the bottom of the lake, and that certain animals or monsters held them there. He at once leaped into the water to rescue them, but immediately the lake overflowed, and increased so prodigiously that it inundated and drowned the whole earth.

Astonished he gave up all thought of his lynxes, and turned his attention to creating the world anew. First he sent a raven to find a small piece of earth with which to build a new world. The raven returned unsuccessful. He made an otter dive down, but he could not reach the bottom. At last a muskrat descended and brought back some earth. With this bit of earth Messou restored everything to its former condition.

But it is among the Iroquois that Great Turtle plays the principal part in the creation; in fact it is said that he upholds the earth to this day.

In one of the cases of the Richmond collection in the museum of the Montgomery County Historical

Cayadutta Creek, Running through the Battlefield of Johnstown.

"Great Spirit"

Society is an old rattle which can be traced back more than a hundred years. We have looked upon it as an interesting relic of the Senecas, a rude musical instrument. It is made from a turtle shell and skin, and in the enclosed space have been placed pebbles for rattles.

But this instrument is interesting beyond all that. Father LeJune, in his Relation of 1639, makes the following statement in describing a dance at a feast given for a sick woman:

> At the head of the procession marched two masters of ceremonies singing and holding the tortoise, on which they did not cease to play. This tortoise is not a real tortoise, but only the shell and skin so arranged as to make a sort of drum or rattle. Having thrown certain pebbles into it they make from it an instrument like that the children in France used to play with. There is a mysterious something, I know not what, in this semblance of a tortoise, to which these people attribute their origin. We shall know in time what there is to it.

It is said that in no Amerind (the word Amerind is a new word coined by the Bureau of Ethnology to take the place of the three words North American Indian: You will notice that it is composed or formed from the first four letters of American and the first three letters of Indian) language could the Jesuit priests find a word to express the idea of God or His attributes. Although the most charitable of people and showing the utmost affection for their children, the Jesuits were unable, in the Amerind language, to impress upon them, or to communicate to them, the idea of an all-loving and charitable Supreme Being. They had their Manitou, but they feared them and gave them the character of the devil, one who should be propitiated by presents, by penances, or by scourges and feasts.

In the Amerind's mind, each animal had a king, as the Great Turtle, the Great Bear, etc. The fathers said to them, "If the animals have each a Supreme Being, why should not man have a great chief of men, who lives in the sky—a Great Spirit?" This idea they accepted, and, although they did not or could not give him the attributes of the Christian's God, the Great Spirit became "a distinct existence, a pervading power in the universe, and a dispenser of justice."

This idea the Jesuits had to accept, although in exceptional cases they seemed to impress their idea of God upon some of their converts while they had them at the missions, but they were sure to become apostates when they returned to their people in the wilderness. So you will see that the "Great Spirit" of the Indians is a modern idea received from the whites and not, as some think, a Supreme Being evolved ages ago from the Amerind mind.

Parkman says:

> The primitive Indians believed in the immortality of the soul, and that skilful hunters, brave warriors, and men of influence went, after death, to the happy hunting-grounds, while the slothful, the cowardly, the weak, were doomed to eat serpents and ashes in dreary and misty regions, but there was no belief that the good were to be rewarded for moral good, or the evil punished for a moral evil.

So you will see that the writing of a history of the Mohawks would be an arduous task: a history filled with mystery and superstition together with kindly

A Colonial Doorway, Guy Park.

deeds and warlike acts; a history of a people endowed with minds that were able to conceive a union of tribes, states, or nations, call them what you may, and to perpetuate that union for centuries, the success of which suggested to our forefathers the union of States, the government under which we now live.

CHAPTER XVIII

EPISODE AT THE SIEGE OF FORT SCHUYLER—THE MURDER OF THE MAIDENS

(" And among the plunder captured by Col. Willett were two fresh scalps with hair smooth and neatly plaited.")

PART I

DURING the year 1754, and previous to the active operations of the last French war, the forts along the Mohawk River were garrisoned by English troops, supplemented occasionally by provincial volunteers. At that time the post at Fort Hunter, although in a dilapidated condition, had a semblance of a garrison in a few soldiers under the command of a young English lieutenant by the name of Robert Stanley, whose headquarters were in an old stone building known as Queen Anne's Chapel parsonage. The soldiers were quartered inside the palisade which enclosed the chapel, and in the chapel itself.

Back of the parsonage to the south extended the primitive forest, with occasional openings made by settlers, partially under cultivation. To the east, west, and north were hundreds of acres of flat lands under cultivation by the Indians and the few white men who constituted the settlement at Tiononderoga. Their nearest neighbor to the east was the family of Jan Wemps, and two miles away on the north bank of

An Episode of Fort Schuyler 199

the Mohawk was the fortified home of Colonel William Johnson, lately named Fort Johnson by its owner. Scattered here and there on the flat lands and the neighboring hills could be seen the rude huts of the Mohawks, with the "long house" near the palisade, also enclosed in a stockade of upright logs set firmly in the ground.

The parsonage was a two-story structure of rough, stone, with deep embrasured windows and small panes of glass protected by heavy wooden shutters, and doors guarded by huge locks with keys large enough for a medieval fortress. Loopholes for the firing of muskets were in evidence in the walls on every side. The interior was divided into four moderate-sized rooms above and below, scantily furnished with rude but substantial furniture. Here Lieutenant Stanley lived, while the household affairs were administered as best they could be by Indian women hired for that purpose. It was a lazy, inactive life that the Lieutenant led, its monotony occasionally broken by visits to the homes of the Johnsons, Wemps, and the Butlers, or an occasional trip down the Mohawk in bateau or canoe to Schenectady for supplies for the garrison.

A year before his regiment had been hurriedly ordered to America he had married a beautiful and loving woman. Two years had passed, but the remembrance of the blissful, tearful good-bye was a sweet memory to him in the wilderness notwithstanding the anguish of separation, and he looked forward with inexpressible longing to the coming June, when she would be with him again. In the meantime he busied himself in brightening the old structure with new bits of furniture and linen for the household, while quick-growing vines were planted in order to cover the weather-stained walls of the gloomy dwelling.

Part II

June has come and with it the ship that bore the wife of Lieutenant Stanley, and on one of those rare days in this leafy month a party is embarking on a well-loaded bateau for a slow voyage up the Mohawk; but with Mr. and Mrs. Stanley are two sturdy children, a boy of seven and a girl of three, whose yellow locks and pink and white complexion seem to indicate that they are of German parentage.

Among the emigrants on board the ship which brought Mrs. Stanley to the shores of America was a frail German with his wife and two children. Before the vessel was many days out, some of the passengers were stricken with a virulent disease, from which many died, among whom were the two Germans spoken of above. The grief of the two children was pitiful, and excited the sympathy of Mrs. Stanley to such an extent that she assumed the care of providing for them in the strange country which they were approaching. For many years it had been the custom for captains of ships plying between the old world and the new to transport emigrants without pay, with the understanding that upon their arrival in port their services should be sold to persons desiring servants, for a sum equalling their passage money, practically making the persons so sold slaves, for a period of years. Lieutenant Stanley, at the request of his wife,

An Episode of Fort Schuyler

purchased the children in this manner, and the boy and girl were indentured to him for a term of ten years.

The bateau on which our party had embarked at Schenectady, although of generous capacity, was heavily loaded with supplies for Fort Johnson, and taxed to the utmost the strength of eight vigorous polemen in making headway against the strong current and over the numerous riffs and shallows between the Kinaquarione hill and Johnson's trading settlement opposite the "painted rocks." At this point, the boat was lightened somewhat by the passengers going ashore and tramping through the forests that fringed the bank of the river.

With much trouble the bateau succeeded in reaching the foot of the riff near the present site of Guy Park; but was unable to proceed any farther, owing to the shallowness of the river between this point and Fort Johnson. Securing the bateau to the north bank and leaving two of their number to watch the cargo, which they had protected with huge tarpaulins, the boat crew, having made packs of some of the portable articles, joined the passengers in the moonlight tramp along the three-mile trail to Fort Johnson. In due time the weary travellers came in sight of the beacon light in the peak of the old stone mansion, supplemented by numerous camp-fires in front of rude Indian camps on the extensive flats in front of the palisaded building.

A Mohawk runner having informed Johnson of the approach of the party, he was at the gate of the stockade to welcome his weary visitors. By his side were his two daughters, Anne and Mary, while in the rear of the family party stood a young woman in semi-barbarous apparel. With raven black hair drawn straight back from her low, smooth brow and fastened in flat plaits on the back of her well-formed head; features comely and complexion a clear olive, tinted on cheek and chin with the warm blood of her dusky race; form of medium height and well rounded with beauty's curves on limb and neck and breast, half-veiled slumbrous eyes and full, crimson lips, she stood apart from the daughters of her lord and master, but with the proud and quiet demeanor that was a marked characteristic in her association with the white guests of Sir William in after years. Dominant and masterful, sensual and affectionate, there is no reason to believe that the Baronet ever regretted the impulse that caused him to select this beautiful Mohawk girl as a successor to his first Indian wife, Caroline, and as stepmother to her own cousins.

After greeting his tired guests the servants were ordered to prepare refreshments for the Lieutenant and his wife, while a motherly black slave took charge of the two forlorn, motherless children.

As commissioner of Indian affairs, Johnson was regarded as an important personage, and frequent visits to Albany and New York, as guest of the wealthy and powerful of those cities, made it necessary that his own household should be ordered on a generous and hospitable plan; therefore the advent of this British officer and his lady in no way disconcerted this lord of the forest lands, who regaled them with all the delicacies of an epicure's larder and the choice liquors of a well-stocked wine cellar.

The advent of an educated English lady into the household of Sir William was of rare occurrence and

Wine Vault Cellar, Old Fort Johnson.

highly appreciated by the Baronet, who was assiduous in his attentions to the officer's wife; she in return regaled her host with news of London and the gossip of the court. Midnight, however, found his guests in slumber, and the early morning, passengers in Indian canoes en route to their home at Fort Hunter.

PART III

Ten years have elapsed since the close of the last chapter and have brought many changes to the family of the Lieutenant, now Captain Stanley. Wounded in the French war at the battle of Lake George, the Captain is now an invalided soldier located at Fort Herkimer. During his residence at Fort Hunter, a daughter was born, and at this period is a beautiful child of nine years. The two German orphans spoken of in the last chapter are still members of his family, sharing the affection of their master, and contributing to his material comfort more as a son and daughter than bondservants. Rudolph, the boy, is a sturdy lad of seventeen and Therese a bright and loving child of thirteen, whose joys and sorrows are mingled with those of her foster sister Mildred.

Life at the old stone manse had been a period of happiness to the young English wife, varied somewhat by anxiety over occasional brawls between the English soldiers and the Mohawks, that sometimes threatened serious consequences, had it not been for the firm hand of their neighbor, Sir William Johnson. At last, however, an outrageous indignity offered to the wife of an Indian chief brought matters to a climax and made it necessary for Sir William to transfer the garrison to some other post and substitute a Colonial squad in place of British soldiers, still retaining Captain Stanley as commandant of the post.

After the hospitable introduction into Sir William's family on the evening of Mrs. Stanley's arrival, visits were frequently exchanged between the two families, resulting in a firm and lasting friendship between the English lady and the dusky Molly Brant, and the comradeship of the motherless half-breeds, Caroline, Charlotte, and William, children of Sir William by his first Indian wife, Caroline, with the German wards of Captain Stanley. The education of Rudolph and Therese had not been neglected and the decade ending in 1765 found them well advanced in studies chosen by the Captain, their teacher, to fit them for the life they were destined to live on the frontier or in their battle with the world at large.

At the age of seventeen Rudolph had grown to be a handsome, robust lad well versed in woodcraft and skill with rifle, taught him by his dusky companions and by experience in the forests which surrounded his chosen home on every side. The necessity of supplying their limited larder with animal food made frequent excursions into the forests unavoidable, and to become a skilful hunter and an expert angler was the ambition of the lads of the frontier settlements.

The French war had practically ended, but the German Flats settlements were frequently alarmed by incursions of small prowling bands of Algonquins from Canada, making it unsafe for unarmed settlers to venture far into the forest without exercising constant vigilance to prevent being surprised by the wily marauders.

An Episode of Fort Schuyler

One of those beautiful days in May when nature seems to entice humanity to enjoy the many attractions of stream and field and forest, two young girls might have been seen in a canoe, venturing from the south shore of the Mohawk River to a small island in mid-stream. The older of the two girls, seated in the bottom of the frail vessel, skilfully handled the paddle as she slowly propelled the frail vessel toward "the haven where they would be," while in the bow reclining, with her tiny hands trailing in the water on each side, was the Captain's daughter, Mildred. Beautiful in form and features, her dark hair clustered around a face ruddy with the hues of perfect health and strength and with all the promises of beautiful and intelligent womanhood.

Therese, her companion and foster sister, is also fair to look upon. Straight of limb and robust in physique as became a forest training almost equal to that of her brother, she also seemed to give assurance of great physical attractions of form and face in early maturity.

Drifting and paddling slowly, the girls directed their canoe to a little cove with shelving beach, and as the bow grated upon the sand were alarmed at the sight of two half-naked Indians who sprang suddenly from the bushes, grasped the canoe on each side and forced it, with its terrified occupants, up the sandy beach and into the low dense thicket of willows that lined the cove. Mildred uttered a wild shriek of terror, which was quickly smothered by the rough hand of one of the savages, and sank into the bottom of the canoe, her terror-stricken face pale and drawn at the horror of the situation. The little German girl still grasped the paddle and gazed stolidly at her captor, as though she failed to comprehend the danger that hovered over them. With a significant touch of the knife at his belt the yound buck grasped the girl, at the same time saying, "Keep still or me kill you," and quickly sped across the small island to the place where their canoe was concealed, followed by his companion carrying the limp form of Mildred and dragging the light canoe with him. Placing one of the girls in each canoe, they hastily covered them with branches of willow, threatening instant death if they stirred or made an outcry, and paddled their boats up the stream and toward the northern shore.

The friendship existing between the members of Captain Stanley's household and Molly Brant and Sir William Johnson's family brought them in contact with Joseph Brant and the half-breed William Johnson of Canajoharie castle at Danube; and after the removal of Captain Stanley to the Herkimer fort, frequent visits were exchanged between the families and the young Indians. It so happened that on the morning of the capture of the two children, Rudolph in company with Tha-yen-da-ne-ga was returning from Indian Castle in a canoe, and, as they were rounding a piece of land a short distance below the island, discovered the Canadian Indians hastily paddling away.

Tha-yen-da-ne-ga's quick eye discovered the war paint of the savages, and at the same time recognized them as Hurons from the vicinity of Quebec; and Rudolph as quickly recognized Therese's canoe, which contained the shivering form of poor Mildred. Shouting the war-cry of the Mohawks, Brant with vigorous strokes of the paddle forced the light vessel

An Episode of Fort Schuyler 207

swiftly in pursuit of the fleeing Hurons, while Rudolph's rifle placed a bullet through the right arm and into the side of the dusky buck in Mildred's canoe, causing him to drop his paddle. At the report of the rifle, the other Huron raised his gun, and as he brought it to rest, and in the act of firing at the pursuers, the little German girl quickly threw herself out of the canoe on the opposite side, clinging to the frail vessel until she capsized it just as the Indian's gun was discharged, the bullet speeding harmlessly toward the zenith instead of the mark of his murderous aim.

The two girls were expert swimmers, and as the Huron was floundering in the water Therese sank into the stream and struck out vigorously, still under the face of the water, towards the advancing canoe. The Huron soon came to the surface, still encumbered with his rifle, and seizing the frail canoe, but keeping it between himself and his approaching enemies, endeavored to reach the north shore of the river.

While this episode was being enacted, a similar one took place in the other canoe, by which the wounded Indian was thrown into the water and Mildred swam fearlessly and rapidly towards the island. Meanwhile the girls' canoe, floating down the stream in the direction of the pursuers, was seized by Therese as she came to the surface a few rods below the place where she had disappeared.

During the floundering of the Indians among the débris of the upturned canoes, Rudolph could not disecovr any trace of his sister after the quick movement that capsized the vessel in which she was concealed, and deeming that she had been wounded and drowned, his rage at the Hurons became intense.

Urging Tha-yen-da-ne-ga to increased exertion he quickly reloaded his rifle, watching keenly the hand of the savage on the canoe which he was using as a shield, in his efforts to reach the north shore that he might escape in the thickets which lined its border. But his struggles were in vain, for at the instant that he sprang from the water's edge to his haven of comparative safety, the unerring bullet from Rudolph's rifle pierced his brain and he sank to the sand, dead. His fatally wounded companion having also disappeared under the waters of the Mohawk, the young men turned their attention toward succoring the recent captives, Tha-yen-da-ne-ga having discovered the perilous situation of Therese in mid-stream, clinging to the capsized canoe, while Mildred was seen lying in a state of collapse on the shore of the island.

The report of the rifles and the war-cry of the Mohawks having alarmed the inhabitants of Fort Herkimer, boats were soon speeding to the scene of disturbance, and many willing hands were ready to offer assistance to the maidens, who proved to be more scared than hurt. Assistance, however, was given to bury the Huron deep in the sands of the shore, unmutilated and uncoffined.

Stopping to pick up Therese and restore the canoe to buoyancy, Brant stepped into the frail vessel and quickly paddled to the fort, while Rudolph hastened to Mildred, whose dripping form was soon nestling in his arms, in perfect comfort and rest, notwithstanding the chill of her involuntary bath and the horror of her brief bondage in the power of the young Hurons.

For many months Mrs. Stanley had been in a

An Episode of Fort Schuyler 209

precarious state of health, notwithstanding the assiduous care of her husband and devoted children; but as the alarm of the garrison over the abduction of the two children was soon communicated to her, she succumbed to the horror of the situation and never recovered consciousness, but passed peacefully away, even amid the joy of the household over the rescue and return of the maidens.

After the death of his wife, Captain Stanley, broken in health and broken-hearted, sent in his resignation to the proper authorities and prepared to take possession of a grant of land which he owned near Fort Stanwix (Rome), and it is here that we find him in 1775, as farmer and successful trader, with warehouses on the trail between the Mohawk and Wood Creek.

Part IV

Although situated on the frontier and a resident of Tryon County for more than twenty years, the Captain was a thorough Briton at heart and loyal to his king; but the sympathies of Rudolph and his sister Therese were with the patriots.

We cannot, however, call the Captain an ardent partisan, for, broken in health and spirit and relying so completely on his adopted son and daughter for the care of his business and his household, he was inclined to remain neutral in the struggle for supremacy that was going on between the patriots and Tories, which kept old Tryon County in a state of turbulency and great unrest for many months.

After the French war and during the era of peace

that prevailed in the valley of the Mohawk subsequent to that event, Rudolph, being fitted for a hunter by training and inclination, spent the greater part of the year in the wilderness, even extending his hunting and trading trips as far west as the Ohio and north and east to the valleys of the St. Lawrence and Lake Champlain, having at times for companions the Oneida half-breed Thomas Spencer, Brant (Thayendanega), and Teg-che-un-to (William Johnson, the half-breed). The young German, being of great physical strength and courage, combined with a cheerful disposition and manly personal beauty, made warm friends among the Palatine settlers and the Iroquois, and was worshipped as almost a god by Mildred and his sister Therese. These two girls had fulfilled the promise of their childhood, and were indeed beautiful in form and features. Many were the suitors that came to the home of Captain Stanley, but, although the friends of the Captain were received with kindness, none were able to make an impression on the hearts of the maidens.

Their education and social standing, as daughter and ward of the British officer, deterred many of the young men of the frontier settlements from offering more than respectful homage to these flowers of the wilderness, and the advances of such men as Walter Butler and Sir John Johnson were early received with such dignity and coldness as to prevent any repetition of attentions other than most respectful. However, the friendships of childhood had continued unbroken between Thayendanega and Rudolph, and the more recent companionship with Thomas Spencer, the young Oneida orator, and Teg-che-un-to the half-

An Episode of Fort Schuyler

breed, made them welcome visitors to the household, and, in the case of Spencer and Brant, honored guests. Although Teg-che-un-to had been admitted as a friend on account of Molly Brant, the young man lacked many of the qualities that bound the trio together. His claim of superiority above the young people of the flats, on account of his left-handed connection with Sir William Johnson and the smattering of an education received at Dr. Wheelock's school at Lebanon, made him disliked, and his general character made him distrusted. Therefore his reception during the later years was more that of suffrance on account of early friendship than any love of the members of Captain Stanley's household for the fellow. An unreasoning jealousy had manifested itself towards Spencer because of the evident pleasure Therese exhibited in the society of the young orator of the forest, on account of his evident loyalty to the whites of the valley, and his power to sway people, both denizens of the wilderness and the whites of the plain, by his eloquence and power of reasoning.

It was Spencer, with the help of Dominie Kirkland, that held the Oneidas to neutrality during the struggle of the patriots for independence and assisted materially in the campaign that turned back St. Leger's hordes to Canada after the unsuccessful siege of Fort Schuyler. The rupture between the two half-breeds finally took place in the spring of 1777, when Tegcheunto declared his love for Therese and urged that she and Mildred should seek protection with the Johnsons at Johnstown. This proposition was rejected by them, and they accepted Spencer's advice to take refuge in Fort Schuyler from the advance of St.

Leger's army. That Spencer loved Therese had been apparent to Rudolph and Mildred for many months, and that Therese also loved the young orator was known to the twain even before the young girl was willing to acknowledge that her desire for his society was any stronger sentiment than that of friendship.

To Rudolph it seemed as though his love for Mildred had no beginning, that he had always loved her. But when in the silence of the forest primeval his thoughts turned to her he knew his passionate, worshipful love sprang to life when he clasped her dripping form to his breast on the island in the midstream and felt her chilled arms around his neck as he murmured "My sweetheart, my love." The awakening of Mildred, however, came to her in her young womanhood, when, on her seventeenth birthday and after an unusually long sojourn in the wilderness, Rudolph returned and met her with a kiss and swift embrace. Then, holding her before him, he looked into her dear eyes and at last found what he had sought for since childhood, the answering, longing love light. It was then, clasped in his arms, that she had met his lips with a clinging, tremulous kiss that told him of the "awakened love that filled her very being."

Part V

Two years have passed, and in the spring of 1777 we find Rudolph enrolled in Colonel Dayton's troops stationed at Fort Dayton, Brant and Tegcheunto in Canada, and Thomas Spencer stirring up the patriots of the Mohawk Valley with the news of the gathering of St. Leger's army at Three Rivers for the proposed expedition against Fort Schuyler.

Killing of the Maidens

It was at this time that Spencer advised and urged Captain Stanley and the two maidens to take refuge in Fort Schuyler from the murderous hordes of St. Leger. The Captain refused to leave his station, but urged and at last commanded the girls to accept the proposition of the young Oneida, saying that, as for him, he was as safe in the camp of the British as in the American fort.

On April 17 and May 3, 1777, troops under Colonel Gansevoort began to arrive at the fort, and on May 28th the remainder of the regiment, under Colonel Willett, making the number of the garrison seven hundred strong; most of whom were soon employed in strengthening the defences and otherwise preparing for the reception of the enemy, who were said to be gathering on the south shore of Lake Ontario near Oswego. With Colonel Willett's troop came Rudolph.

Alarmed at the various rumors of the gathering of the forces of the English and the barbarity of Indians, who with their families constituted the major part of the expedition of St. Leger, many non-combatants found refuge inside of the fortifications, among whom were a woman and two children, the eldest being a bright young girl of sixteen, named Nellie Earle. Mildred, Therese, and Nell soon became inseparable companions and leaders in many innocent sports that were inaugurated to enliven the tedium of the limited quarters that constituted their temporary abode. Accustomed as the trio were to frontier life, one of their chief pleasures was in morning rambles outside of the fortification but within the line of out-sentinels or pickets that encircled the fort, closely watching for evidence of the approach of the enemy.

The siege of Fort Schuyler and the attendant battle of Oriskany, together with the battle of Bennington, which turned the tide of war and led on to the defeat and surrender of General Burgoyne's army at Saratoga, are well known to students of history, but it may be well to outline the situation of affairs in the Mohawk Valley at the period of which I am writing, July 27, 1777.

General Herkimer, with the assistance of Thomas Spencer, had succeeded in arousing the patriots of the Mohawk Valley to the gravity of the situation, and was rapidly gathering the hardy yeomanry of the frontier at Fort Dayton for the relief of Fort Schuyler, which was threatened with investment and capture by St. Leger, whose army was slowly advancing from Oswego. With the British forces under command of Colonel Barry St. Leger were a detachment of British regulars, a band of Tories under Sir John Johnson and Colonel John Butler, and a large body of Canadian Indians and the disaffected of the Iroquois, under Colonel Daniel Claus and Captain Joseph Brant (Thayendanega).

No evidence of Indian scouts had been seen in the vicinity of Fort Schuyler, but a small working party from the fort had been attacked by a party of Amerinds near Fort Newport on Wood Creek, and some of the soldiers killed and others taken prisoners. In order to protect the men at work, a party of one hundred of the garrison as guard, among whom was Rudolph, were sent out in the early hours of the morning with a tearful "God speed" from Mildred and Therese.

After the departure of the guard, the trio wandered

Killing of the Maidens

aimlessly out of the fort, going in the opposite direction from that taken by the soldiers, and soon came to the picket line; and in the same listless manner, picking berries and wild flowers as they went, out into the woods, unmindful of lurking foes.

The three maidens, fresh from their morning ablutions, were attired in short, dark blue cotton skirts, with low-cut blouse of white linen shirred across the neck, and short loose sleeves, exposing the firm health-tinted flesh of neck and shoulders, while their feet were encased in neatly fitting buckskin moccasins, laced half way to the knee. The long brown hair of Nellie, the black tresses of Mildred, and the golden locks of blonde Therese were braided in glossy plaits, which hung below their waists, while each maiden carried a stout staff.

Mildred, the life of the party, was tall and lithe of limb, with that pure white complexion which might well be called transparent, barely concealing as it did the ruddy hue of health that seems ready to bloom on cheek and chin to match the full red lips, seemingly forever parted for pensive smile or gay peal of laughter. Her eyes, whose long lashes and brows were as midnight in blackness, were of that uncertain tint of dark gray, shaded to deepest olive, which unfolds to you the heart that the eye of black seems to hide as with a mask.

Both Therese and Mildred had blossomed into beautiful womanhood, although inured to the hardships and toils of frontier life, and the sports of stream, field, and forest had given them strength of limb that many a college athlete might envy.

Reclining under the shade of a small cluster of

forest trees, the two older girls were thinking of the loved ones and the dangers that encompassed them, and listlessly watching Nell, who had wandered a short distance from them in search of forest flowers, when they were startled by the appearance of an Indian in hideous war-paint, and the piercing cry of terror from Nell as the savage seized her as she turned for flight. Springing to their feet, Therese, followed by Mildred, rushed to the assistance of their companion, who was pinioned against a tree with one hand of the Indian, while with the other he drew his knife. As he raised to strike, Therese, who was in advance, brought her stout staff down on his head, crushing the skull and laying him dead at her feet. Almost at the instant of the stroke that killed the savage the two brave girls found themselves in the grasp of two of his companions, while Nell, released and slightly wounded, sped with the fleetness of a deer towards the fort, a half a mile away.

Pausing an instant when she found she was not pursued, she saw the hatchet and scalping-knife do their deadly work on the prostrate forms of her companions and then with even greater speed continued her flight until she fell unconscious at the open portal of the fort.

It afterwards transpired that on the evening of the day of this atrocious murder the assassins were boasting in the presence of Thayendanega and Tegcheunto of the slaying of the maidens. The description that the two Hurons gave of their victims attracted the chief's attention and he ordered them to lead him to the spot, Tegcheunto accompanying him, and was horrified to find the mangled bodies

Killing of the Maidens

of their two friends. With a calmness that was marvellous in one of so passionate a nature, Brant ordered the bodies placed on a litter and carried to a secluded spot outside of the encampment. A grave was prepared and with simple ceremonies by the army chaplain, and wrapped in the blankets of Brant and William, the bodies of the friends of their youth and manhood were lowered in the grave.

Twenty-four hours after, the bodies of the two Hurons were found outside of the camp, bearing the same wounds that they had inflicted upon their victims.

The grief of Rudolph, when, upon his return from Wood Creek the day after the occurrence, Nell Earle related to him the terrible affair, was grievous to behold.

With the consent of Colonel Gansevoort, Rudolph asked for volunteers to go in search of the bodies, but was somewhat embarrassed by the large number who were eager to join in the perilous attempt. Selecting, however, three trusty scouts, he, following the explicit directions given him by Nell, found the spot, plainly indicated by gruesome evidence and the blood-stained staff of Therese.

The utmost wariness and circumspection had been necessary in order to reach the spot, which was on the outskirts of one of the Indian encampments west of the fort, and indicated on some old maps as "the scalping tree." A few rods north could be seen the straggling camp-fires of the Indians, while to the south lay the cedar swamp. The sight of the staff brought vividly to mind the courageous attempt of the young girls to rescue their companion and their horrible death by their cruel captors. Evidence was plainly visible that they did not yield up their young lives without a fearful struggle with these ghouls of the forest lands.

Terrible rage filled the breast of Rudolph, but it was of that calm and deliberate character that boded ill to the persons who were the occasion of it. The flickering light of the camp-fires was but a few rods away, and a shot from a rifle would undoubtedly result in death or capture. The young man did not fear death, but rather welcomed the thought of the cessation of life, the eternal lapse of memory; but did not care to give his life for one or even two of the hated race that had brought this great grief upon him. In his rage he said that scores of lives could not atone for their murder, and he determined to take care of his own life that he might wreak terrible vengeance on the dusky warriors of the tribe of Hurons. The presence of members of the hated race, however, so near the spot of the brutal attack was an incentive for instant action.

During consultation in regard to the plan of attack, Rudolph insisted that he should warily approach one of the outlying camps alone, the others to follow near enough to support him with their rifles if it should be necessary for him to make a hurried retreat.

Concealing themselves at a distance that rendered the movements in camp distinctly visible in the light of the many fires, they waited impatiently until the occupants of the wigwams should seek rest on their rude couches, often only mother earth. It is a singular fact that the Indians seldom protected their camps with sentinels or outposts, but trusted to their own wakefulness to guard against surprises, even when on the war-path. Knowing this custom, the scouts had but little fear of being discovered after evidence of activity had ceased.

The wigwam which had been selected as the object of attack lay outside the circle of light, and the savages had gradually retired from the great central fire, leaving but one dusky warrior sitting on the ground clasping his knees while he listlessly watched the dying embers. Rudolph's party drew stealthily near until they could discern the dark forms of two warriors in slumber outside of the weather-stained canvas of their tepee. Motioning the scouts to halt at a little elevation which concealed their forms when lying at full length, Rudolph continued to advance, prone upon his stomach, with the sinuous motion of a huge reptile, until he could distinguish the features of his intended victims. Slowly circling around until he approached the heads of the sleeping warriors, who were lying parallel with each other, he raised himself on one knee and with two rapid strokes of his hunting hatchet cleft the brain of each dusky foe, without a sound except a guttural exclamation from his last victim, which aroused the watcher at the fire. Starting to his feet, the savage stood in a listening attitude only to receive the deadly stroke from a hatchet hurled with unerring precision by one of Rudolph's companions, the force of the weapon piercing his brain and laying him at full length on the glowing coals. Retreating as silently as they had advanced, the scouting party arrived at the fort in the early hours of the morning.

On August 2d and 3d St. Leger's whole army

arrived and completely invested the fort, the Indians especially annoying the garrison by a continual firing of small arms, at times skulking through the underbrush and potato vines of a large cultivated field in the immediate vicinity of the fortifications, on the west. During this period Rudolph seemed tireless, and was ever at his post to pick off any of his hated foes who were unfortunate enough to expose any portion of their dusky naked bodies to the unerring aim of his trusty rifle. So careless of exposure had he become that he received a reprimand from Col. Willett, who ordered him to keep under cover, as the small garrison could ill spare so brave a soldier and such an unerring marksman. If any particularly hazardous work was to be done, Rudolph was always the first to volunteer, at times heedlessly exposing himself as though fearless of death. From a happy-go-lucky good fellow, with kindly, cheerful disposition, he had become silent and moody, at times standing for hours at a casement with set teeth and eager eyes watching for an opportunity to wreak vengeance on any of the dusky race who had inflicted this great sorrow upon him. As yet he did not know that the murderers had been slain by his old-time friends Thayendanega and Tegcheunto, and his only thought seemed to be to kill, kill, in hopes that his bullet might reach the heart of the assassins. Although tenderly attached to little Nell, who lay wounded in the southwest bomb-proof, he refrained from visiting her often, knowing that he would lose command of himself in her presence and probably retard her recovery from an excess of emotion. Withdrawing himself from his friends and

Killing of the Maidens

left alone with his grief and his rage, he seemed to develop savage instincts that were entirely foreign to his nature. He became, in fact, a monomaniac, crouching here and there, starting at the least sound, while his wild gaze sought the forest and the low shrubs in the direction of the Indian encampments. At times his eager face would put on a grim smile as his keen eye caught the waving motion of the feathers of a scalp lock or the bronze hand of an Indian putting aside a branch, in his stealthy advance towards the fort to pick off some careless picket or fearless soldier, and he became at once the wary marksman of the forest, keenly watching his foe and luring him on by careless indifference to his exposure until with quick movement and apparently without an aim of precision his rifle's missile found its way to the life-blood of his foe.

At last, on the 6th day of August, came word that General Herkimer was advancing to the relief of the garrison with nine hundred eager and impetuous patriots, with the request that when the messengers arrived at the fort, Colonel Gansevoort should make a sortie in order to draw the attention of the British and Indians from their advance and make it easier for his (Herkimer's) troops to enter the fort.

But General Herkimer was checked by that fearfully fatal ambuscade of Brant's at Oriskany, which resulted in a hand-to-hand battle of many hours' duration and the dearly-bought victory of the patriots of the Mohawk Valley, who were left in possession of the field of battle, with one third of their comrades lying dead and wounded and their loved General seriously injured.

With St. Leger's troops at Oriskany were Brant and Tegcheunto, the half-breed, and with the patriots Thomas Spencer, the Oneida. During the latter part of the engagement, personal encounters frequently took place between former neighbors, sometimes the only weapon a knife, and frequently with bare hands.

In the midst of the fray, however, Thomas Spencer found himself confronted by Tegcheunto armed with knife and tomahawk and evidently intent upon taking his life. Thomas was armed with knife only, although supplemented with brawny hands and muscles of steel, as became a man who had followed the trade of blacksmith for a number of years. It was at the time the retreating cry of "Oonah, Oonah!" was given, and the Indians were fast withdrawing from the conflict, that Spencer, greatly wearied, was resting on a log where the plateau drops to the north and finally ends in a swamp, when he heard the breaking of a twig behind him, Springing to his feet, he turned just in time to intercept a blow from a tomahawk in the hand of young Johnson, by grasping the handle as it descended.

The struggle for the weapon was brief and it was soon lying in a thicket a few feet away. As the hatchet disappeared, each man drew his knife and, taking a step backward, watched his adversary for the first movement of attack.

Tegcheunto, with the blood of King Hendrick and Sir William Johnson in his veins, was no mean adversary to the young blacksmith, whose lithe, sinewy form was a few inches taller than the broad-shouldered half-breed. The place where they had met was a level plateau sparsely covered with forest trees of great girth, with here and there the forms of dead and wounded American and British soldiers and Indian warriors, with red, green and blue garments mingled with dusky flesh, gaudy trappings and feathered head-dresses. A little farther to the south could be seen other combatants, some in the close embrace of a death struggle, others in retreat and pursuit.

The sight of the man who had gained the love of the maiden who had spurned him, and the temporary advantage Spencer had gained by disarming him of his tomahawk, roused the revengeful blood of the savage to furious rage, and muttering between his set teeth, "You d—d dog of an Oneida, I'll send you where your yellow-haired sweetheart has gone," he made a vicious lunge at his exposed side, which would have ended the blacksmith's life had it not been for a quick spring to the right, and the momentum of the blow, which threw Johnson off his guard.

Before he could recover, Spencer drove his knife to the hilt in his brawny breast, coolly withdrawing the same, as his foe fell backwards, adding one more to the long list of dead on Oriskany's battle-field.

While these scenes were being enacted at Oriskany, Colonel Willett was making the sortie from Fort Schuyler asked for by General Herkimer. With Willett's detachment went Rudolph. The impetuous charge of the Americans drove in the pickets and dispersed the advance guard before it could be formed for resistance, and they sought safety in flight. Two encampments of the Indians were totally routed and many wagon loads of supplies and baggage were brought into the fort, together with blankets, kettles, Indian trinkets and garments thrown off by the Indians who were engaged in the battle at Oriskany, and five British standards. Great joy was manifested by the garrison over the success of the raid and the plunder secured. Among the various articles found in the Indians' camp were two fresh scalps. One of the scalps was of golden hair, the other glossy black, and evidently those of Mildred and Therese Stanley; neatly braided and smoothly dressed as they wore it the morning they wandered out to meet their dreadful death.

The effect of the discovery upon Rudolph can better be imagined than described. The long-pent-up tears that flowed, the only relief to a heart surcharged with grief, rage and remorse, left this strong man utterly prostrate, refusing food and declining to perform those duties which had been eagerly welcomed since the day of their disappearance.

On the third day after the sortie he appeared again on the ramparts, heedlessly exposing himself to the fire of the enemy as though he courted death as the only relief from his sufferings.

All night the British bombarded the fort, and all night long Rudolph with rifle across his arm, paced the ramparts, while shells were exploding all about him. But just as the eastern sky changed its hue and put on the gray livery of dawn, a shot from the enemy pierced the heart already broken with grief, and Rudolph died, murmuring with his faintest breath, "Sweetheart! sister!"

Club House of "The Antlers."

CHAPTER XIX

A VISIT TO DADANASCARA, THE SUMMER HOME OF ALFRED DE GRAFF—CHARMING VIEWS AND HISTORIC SCENES THEREABOUT—ANCIENT INDIAN CAMP ON THE VROOMAN FARM REVISITED

PERHAPS there is no book that was ever written in which scenes of the historic Mohawk Valley have been described, or tragic events related, either of fact or fiction, that has given more pleasure to the inhabitants of that immense tract of forests and plains, hills, valleys, and streams, hissing cataracts and purling brooks, once called Tryon County, than Harold Frederic's *In the Valley*.

It is almost impossible to wander far afield either north or west in the vicinity of old Mount Johnson, or Fort Johnson as it was renamed in 1757, without trying to locate a trail, or waterfall, or gloomy gulf where the black boy Tulp was dashed crashing to the rocks below, or to find the secluded council glen of the Mohawks, so graphically described. And although we have been informed by the writer himself that his scenes and incidents were all imaginary, and that he never passed through the "Valley" until three years after the publication of his book, we like to hide that statement away back in some remote cell of the brain, dormant, and go on dreaming of sylvan nooks and gloomy gulfs peopled with a real black boy and Philip Cross, Daisy Stewart, and the generous, sturdy young Douw.

The last day in June, 1905, was one of the rare days of which poets sing, one of the days that seem to appeal irresistibly to the lover of nature to wander in haunts primitive and to forget, if possible, all things urban. Yielding to such appeal our trio of congenial spirits alighted from the suburban trolley at Getman's Crossing *en route* for Dadanascara. Shunning the highways, we took a cut cross-country traversing swampy lands, tangled woods, fields cultivated and uncultivated, sometimes passing through fields of white daisies and yellow marguerites and purple clover blossoms as high as the waist, again threading among stumps and boulders and over turf as grateful to tired feet as a velvet carpet, and at last, under the grateful shade of lofty pines and stunted hemlock and cedar, arrived at the cliff of the Dadanascara.

Here my attention was called to a well-graded and well-defined road-bed, following the course of the creek, gradually descending until it reaches its bed and by a ford crosses it to the western or northern bank.

Our objective point being Dadanascara, the country home of Alfred De Graff, a mile away, we did not, at that time, descend to the bed of the stream, but continued on our way along the edge of the cliff, with an occasional glance at the bed of

A Visit to Dadanascara

the gulf, nearly seventy feet below. Following a lane evidently used for cattle we soon emerged from the wood and found ourselves on the edge of the 600-feet plateau and 300 feet above the wide expanse of flat lands that stretches out from the N. Y. C. R. R. to the banks of the Mohawk. The view of the hills of Florida and Glen from this point is entrancing. At our feet, although a half-mile away, is the wide blue ribbon of the river, a fitting border to the waving fields of grain that spread before us east, west, and south, an unbroken expanse of the yellow-green of its vernal bloom.

On the south side of the Mohawk lie before us, *en panorama*, the Florida hills in all their beauty of emerald hues, and the clear air discloses to us in turn Fort Hunter, nestling by the turbulent Schoharie, the Jesuit shrine Auriesville, and a little farther, and on top of the plateau, the little village of Glen, while along the southwestern horizon are seen in the dim distance the Schoharie highlands and the Helderberg Mountains. Overhead, the blue sky is luminous with light and heat, while the distant horizon is outlined with cumulus clouds of ponderous size, each gray convolution bordered with a snow-white lining which shines like silver in the declining sun.

Descending the hill we turned to the west and on a slight elevation we saw Dadanascara—not the creek, but the beautiful country place so named by its owner, Alfred De Graff. One of the trio expressed the thought of the others when he exclaimed, "The most beautiful country home in the Mohawk Valley!"

Embowered in trees of generous growth, and with tasteful out-buildings scattered here and there, a full and uninterrupted view of the dwelling is impossible. But in that fact lies one of its chief charms. As we wander about the spacious lawn, new vistas of beauty meet the eyes at almost every step as the creamy white of the structure becomes visible through the foliage, which half conceals yet half reveals new charms both picturesque and beautiful.

But our quest was not yet ended, and we reluctantly turned from the courteous attention of Mr. Howard De Graff to explore the gulf of Dadanascara. One of our party remained to finish a bottle of "Schlitz," but the others hurried on. As soon as the tardy one joined us he reported that he had seen three snakes in a pool we had just passed. Of course he thought we believed him, but we kept wondering how three snakes could be produced from one small bottle of "Schlitz."

And then the professor told about a young man coming in late to a ball with a big jag on, who stepped up to the leader of the orchestra and asked, "Was that Tannhäuser you just played?" "No," replied the leader, "It was Anheuser." As the crowd laughed he turned away, saying to the leader, "You're all right." Another true story was told: A popular Division Street grocer had shaven off his mustache. An Italian customer came into the store and at once noticed the smooth face of the grocer, and, wanting to tell him he looked like a clergyman, he began, "You looka like, you looka,

Abandoned Highway to Albany.   Leading to Dadanascara Ford.

A Visit to Dadanascara

you looka," but the word he wanted would not present itself. All at once his face lighted up as he said, "You looka—you looka like a church."

But if we stop to tell stories we will never get through the chasm.

We had descended into the bed of the creek immediately north of a substantial iron bridge spanning the stream for farm purposes. About 200 feet from this point the slate cliffs appear, hemming in the stream for nearly a mile and a half, their perpendicular heights of perhaps seventy feet making a barrier all of that distance that is impossible to scale, so that a person entering this slaty gorge must go through to the end or return from whence he came. The bed itself, about fifty feet wide, is flat and extends close to the cliffs, so that in ordinary high water it is impossible to make the trip dry-shod.

This chasm is one of the most picturesque of the Mohawk Valley and only needs to be seen to be appreciated. Each high cliff is crowned with forest growths close to its edge, the tall pines adding forty feet or more to the seeming height of the barriers by which we are hemmed in.

I have called this spot a chasm, gorge, and gulf, but I think it will bear the importation of the western name of canyon to fittingly describe its appearance. The irregular slaty cliffs with their black slaty scales piled in myriads of layers and festooned from above with wild grape vines, the hardy honeysuckle, and poison ivy, show signs of erosion and corrasion and suggest post-glacial origin. At a point about half a mile from the upper end of the canyon the creek makes two sharp turns in the form of a letter S, the cliffs being worn into semicircles by the action of the water, leaving but a narrow sloping ridge, with a very precarious foothold, between the pool at its base and the rocky amphitheatre. In fact at this point I lost my grip on the slimy slate and slipped into the pool.

Sitting on a narrow ledge at the foot of the cliff and gazing at the highest point of the precipice on the opposite bank, I could not blame the careless reader of *In the Valley* for selecting this point as the spot from which Philip Cross threw the black boy to seeming death, and the later tragedy where the crazy Tulp seeks revenge, and, with his enemy, finds death on the rocky bed below.

Still dreaming I see the bloody battle-field of Oriskany, and in the bright moonlight that followed that dreadful day can discern the wounded Philip Cross, placed in the birchen canoe for its five days' journey down the Mohawk River, floating noiseless by night through the narrow canalized stream, with barely water enough to float the heavily laden canoe, past the wide and wondrously beautiful valley of the German Flats, over the difficult portage of the falls, and among its picturesque rocky islets, and finally on the long, smooth stretches of quiet waters, guided by the silent, slow, and skilful movement of the paddle in the hands of Douw as he watches his dying enemy.

Aroused from reverie he notes the silvery light of the full moon and its shimmering reflection in the placid river and becomes aware, by the wide reaches

Dadanascara Gorge.

A Visit to Dadanascara

of flat lands on the left bank, that he is nearing the end of his journey on the river.

Guiding his frail canoe towards the shore, he searches for and soon finds the entrance to the Dadanascara, up which he slowly paddles nearly to the cliffs, where he finds his companion, Enoch Wade, waiting for him. And I almost expect to see the slow approach of the boatmen with the canoe on their shoulders around the bend below. The splash of a stone thrown into the pool at my feet arouses me, and the vision vanishes.

A few rods further on, at another bend of the stream, the cliffs fall away and we reach the open fields again. And here we meet again the road we spoke of before, leading to a ford which connects, a hundred feet farther up the stream, with a well-defined road, and further on a branch road with a westward trend. This road and ford antedate the Schenectady and Utica turnpike built by Seth Whitmore, Osias Bronson, and others in the year 1800. One of these roads was the main road to the West, and the other an old road to Johnstown. A bridge may have spanned the stream, but at present there is an easy ford across the slate bed of the canyon, which was probably used by Sir John Johnson and his Tories and Indians in his raid of the valley, and his approach to the house of Colonel Visscher was probably through the canyon of the Dadanascara.

You will remember the story:

Shortly after midnight of the 22d of May, 1780, the Visscher mansion was assailed by a combined force of the Tory and Indian foe. The inmates consisted of the Colonel, his mother, his sisters, two brothers, and the servants, who were subjected to the bloody violence of more than a hundred enemies. The scene which followed was one too deeply imbued with horror to be attempted in this brief recital. The sisters fled, seeking concealment in the gloom of the gorge of the Dadanascara Creek, while the mother, feeble with age and crippled by disease, was unable to move. The three brothers, John, Harman, and the Colonel, engaged in hand-to-hand combat in defence of their home and mother, but were overpowered. The first two were murdered and scalped, and the latter was also (as was thought) among the slain. He was scalped and left for dead, after which the house was pillaged and then fired—the enemy departing amid the blaze. The Colonel, however, revived, and recovered sufficient strength not only to escape the flames, but also to drag away the bloody corpses of his brothers. His mother had survived a savage blow, and he was able to carry her to a place of safety.

These statements indicate a degree of nerve that seems almost incredible, but they were among the facts of history. Colonel Visscher afterwards found shelter among his friends in Schenectady. His murdered brothers were buried in one grave near their father in the family cemetery, and Colonel Visscher was the sole male survivor of the line. He recovered his health and immediately resumed active service.

The house which was burned stood nearer the turnpike than the present De Graff mansion, its exact site being indicated by the bronze deer in front of the house.

After the war of the Revolution the Colonel rebuilt his family mansion on the spot where the De Graff mansion now stands, in a very solid and spacious manner. After many years it was again enlarged and beautified by the present owner, Mr.

A Visit to Dadanascara

Alfred De Graff, who represents the fifth generation in direct line of succession from Colonel Visscher.

After we reached the ford the writer did not have much assistance from his companions in locating roads, owing to the fact that their love for the good things of the woods and fields outweighed their love for history, and they spent their time in tickling their palates with strawberries and squaw-berries, wintergreens and calamus roots.

After emerging entirely into the open fields we found the Dadanascara wandering at all points of the compass, carving its bed through the fertile fields of the north. The stream seemed to be at the bottom of an extended valley, or rather the bed of a large prehistoric lake whose water had, in ages past, carved its way through a slaty barrier and formed an outlet through the canyon of the Dadanascara.[1]

But all things come to an end, and the lengthening shadows of the sun emphasized the fact that our ramble must end; but we could not resist the desire to revisit an old Indian camp on the Vrooman farm and were rewarded with a handful of prehistoric relics, although we barely caught our trolley.

[1] (Query: Did not the Sacandaga flow south into the Mohawk before the ice cap of the glacial period had receded far enough so that the water of that river and the prehistoric Vlaie Lake could make its present connection with the Hudson River?)

INDEX

A

Abe, Little, 21, 74, 78, 80
Abeel, John, 175, 176
Abercrombie, Gen., 38, 127
Abraham, Chief, 20, 23
Adageghteinge patent, 156
Adams, Robert, 157, 159, 160
Adams, William, 159, 160
Adariaghta, 8
Adirondack, 27
Adriutha, 8
Agniers, 28
Akin, Ethan, 165
Albany, 52, 67, 73, 113, 137
Algonquin, 27
Allen, Ethan, 38
Alter, N. Burton, 184
Amherst, Gen. Jeffrey, 38
Anderson, Lieut., 98
Andiatarocte, 27
Andrustown, 105
Arnold, General Benedict, 87, 98, 99, 101, 102, 103, 104
Atayataronghte, Louis, 114, 115, 116, 118
Auriesville, 227

B

Babbington Patent, 158
Ball, Lieut., 88
Barclay, Rev. James, 10
Batten Kil, 80
Bellem, Major, 89
Bellinger, Col., 93
Bellinger Family, 124
Benschoten, Captain, 89, 118
Bird, Col., 79
Bloody Pond, 36, 59
Bonney, Mrs., 147
Boquet, Col. Henry, 42, 43, 51
Bowen, Henry, 186
Bowen, Lieut., 88
Bowen, William, 186
Bradstreet, Gen. John, 59, 127

Brant, Joseph, (Thayendanega), 21, 50, 59, 66, 73, 74, 75, 76, 78, 79, 103, 109, 111, 114, 117, 118, 119, 120, 122, 137, 143, 206, 207, 208, 209, 210, 211, 214, 221, 222
Brant, Molly, 11, 20, 21, 22, 74, 78, 79, 80, 137, 149, 150, 153, 158, 202, 204, 206, 211
Brant, Nicklaus, 23
Brantford, 143
Brant, Young, 151
Bronson, Osias, 231
Brown, Col. John, 112, 115, 152
Brown, John, 170
Bruyas, Father, 28
Boyne, 2
Buell, Augustus C., 5
Burgoyne, Gen. John, 38, 80, 83, 84, 93, 103, 105, 214
Burke, Joe, 17
Bushy Run, 39, 43
Butler, Col. John, 66, 77, 84, 92, 93, 99, 100, 121, 138, 159, 214
Butler's Mills, 120
Butler's Rangers, 22, 111, 116
Butler, Lieut. Walter, 66, 100, 101, 103, 210
Byrne, Michael, 6, 7, 9, 22
Byrne, William, 157

C

Cadogan's Horse, 5
Campbell, Daniel, 152, 158
Campbell, Sir Colin, 58, 59
Canajoharie, 108, 109, 171
Carlingford, 6
Caroline (Hendrick), 5, 11, 21, 22, 23, 75, 202
Caroline Jr. (Johnson), 20, 22, 204
Cassidy, Luke, 91
Catskill Mountains, 182
Caughnawaga, 174
Caughnawagas, 29, 30, 62, 87, 88, 89, 112, 143
Champlain, 27, 28

Index

Champlain, Lake, 12, 26, 29, 30, 31, 38
Charlotte (Johnson), 20, 22, 204
Charlotte River, 156
Cherry Valley, 101, 105, 120
Chew, Joseph, 157, 159, 160
Chew, William, 157
Claus, Col. Daniel, 15, 58, 62, 66, 100, 103, 150, 158 160, 161, 214
Claus, William, 158
Clinton, Gen. James, 107, 109
Clinton, Gov. George, 116
Cobleskill, 108
Cochran, Maj., 86, 98, 99
Colbraith, William, 81
Colbraith, Lieut., 81
Committee of Safety, 64, 66, 73, 172
Cooper, J. Fenimore, 27
Conowaroharie, 120
Cornplanter, 111, 175, 176
Cox, Col. Ebenezer, 64, 75, 76
Creation, Legends of, 189
Crogan, George, 14, 50, 51
Cross, Philip, 225, 230
Crown Point, 12, 29, 31, 38
Cuyler, Jacob C., 16
Cuyler, John, 16

D

Dadanascara, 225-233
Daly, Patrick, 157
Danube, 78, 79
Davidson, Dr. Oliver, 16
Dayton, Col. Elias, 67, 83, 138
Dease, Dr. John, 156, 159, 166
De Courcelle, 28
De Graff, Alfred, 226, 227, 233
De Graff, Howard, 228
De Lancey, Hon. James, 7, 13
De Lancey, Stephen, 7
Delaney, Col., 127
De Levy, M., 82
Delawares, 42, 45, 46, 51, 52
De Peyster, Abraham, 169
De Peyster, Maj.-Gen. J. Watts, 56, 142, 147, 165, 166, 168, 169
Deseronto, 21, 143
Detroit, 40, 42, 45, 46, 47, 59
Devil's Hole, 39, 48, 49, 50
Dewitt, Captain, 89
Diefendorf Family, 124
Diefendorf, Frederick, 124
Diefendorf, Jacob, 124, 129

Diefendorf, Lieut., 88, 91
Dieskau, Baron de, 29, 31, 32, 34, 35, 36
Dorlack, 123, 124, 127, 129
Douw, Volkert T., 106
Doxtader (Tory), 123, 125
Drogheda, 2, 3
Duane, James, 106
Dubois, Col., 115, 117, 118
Duncan, Captain, 111, 112
Dunmore's War, 15

E

Earle, Nellie, 213, 215, 217
Edward, Fort, 30, 32
Elimore, Col., 70, 86, 87

F

Fisher, Col., 188
Fisher, Herman, 188
Fisher, John, 188
Florida, 16
Folsom, Captain, 36
Fonda, Adam, 188
Fonda, Major Jelles, 71, 112, 159
Fort Bull, 82, 88
Fort Constitution, 128
Fort Dayton, 83, 87, 89, 100, 101, 102, 130, 131, 132, 133, 212, 214
Fort Frontenac, 127
Fort Hunter, 8, 74, 77, 78, 112, 121, 143, 182, 183, 184, 198, 203, 227
Fort Keyser, 113
Fort Lyman, 30, 31, 32, 35, 36
Fort Newport, 82, 88, 89, 98, 214
Fort Paris, 112, 113
Fort Pitt, 42, 44, 46, 51
Fort Plain, 108, 112, 115, 116, 125, 127, 130, 175
Fort Plank, 120
Fort Rensselaer, 123
Fort Schlosser, 49
Fort Schuyler, 61, 70, 79, 82, 83, 84, 86, 87, 88, 100, 101, 102, 104, 105, 106, 119, 120, 129, 144, 145, 198, 211, 212, 214, 223
Fort Stanwix, 82, 83, 127, 209
Fort Ticonderoga, 31, 37, 38, 127
Fort William, 82
Fraught, Dr., 130
Frey, Barent, 66, 93
Frey, Henry, 159

Index

G

Gansevoort, Col. Peter, 84, 85, 86, 87, 90, 93, 95, 104, 107, 127, 213, 217, 221
Gansevoort, Lendert, 177
Garoga Creek, 115
Genealogy of the Johnson Family, 161, 164
Genesee Valley, 106
George, Lake, 13, 17, 27, 28, 29, 30, 31, 32, 36, 37, 59
German Flats, 12, 45, 48, 98. 105, 120, 128, 129, 130, 152
Getman, Captain, 132
Getman's Crossing, 226
Gladwin, Major, 40, 41, 42
Glen-Sanders House, 81, 85
Glen Sanders, Leenderte, 85, 86
Gordon, Lord Adam, 57
Gort, William, 187
Gorvel, Ensign, 156
Goupil, Réné, 28
Grand River, Canada, 21
Grant, Mrs. Julia, 22
Grant, Mrs., of Laggan, 52, 57, 65
Griggs, Captain, 88, 95
Groot, Philip, 8
Gross, Captain, 124, 125
Guy Park, 66, 175, 201

H

Haldiman, Gov. Frederick, 121
Halsey, Francis W., 69, 70
Hanser, Henry, 187
Hanson, J. Howard, 172
Hanson Patent, 174
Harper, Col. John, 71, 73
Harper, Col. William, 116
Harpersfield, 72
Hartley, Martin J., 184
Havelock, General, 59
Hendrick, King, 11, 13, 20, 23, 32, 33, 222
Herkimer, 130
Herkimer, Han Yost, 66
Herkimer, Gen. Nicholas, 64, 70, 74, 75, 76, 77, 78, 84, 85, 91, 92, 153, 155, 214, 221, 223
Hewitt, J. N. B., 190
Hicks, Mayor Whitehead, 127
Hoffman's Ferry, 28
Hoofe, Henry, Patent, 175
Horicon, Lake, 27

Howe, Gen. Sir William, 83, 84,
Huger, Captain, 42
Hurons, 27, 28, 45

I

Ibbit, Moses, 159, 160
Indian Castle, 70, 79, 117, 137
Iroquois, 11, 20, 27, 29, 30, 50, 65, 105
Iroquois Lake, 27, 28
Irving, Washington, 135
Iscariot, Judas, 55

J

Jogues, Isaac, 27, 28
Johnson, Anna, 10, 57, 158, 161, 201
Johnson, Anne Brant, 154, 155
Johnson, Catherine Maria, 142
Johnson, Christopher, 5
Johnson, Mrs. Christopher, 139
Johnson, George, 154
Johnson, Col. Guy, 15, 24, 62, 65, 73, 74, 119, 137, 145, 150, 158, 160, 161
Johnson, James Stephen, 142
Johnson, John, 155, 158
Johnson, Sir John, 10, 14, 15, 16, 56, 57, 59, 60, 62, 63, 64, 65, 66, 81, 84, 99, 100, 103, 104, 111, 112, 113, 114, 116, 117, 118, 119, 121, 122, 134, 137, 141, 142, 143, 144, 145, 150, 151, 156, 157, 158, 159, 160, 161, 186, 187, 188, 210, 214, 231
Johnson, Magdalene, 153, 154
Johnson, Margaret, 154
Johnson, Mary, 10, 57, 58, 150, 158, 161, 201
Johnson, Peter, 21, 66, 150, 153, 156
Johnson, Lady Polly Watts, 16, 67, 134, 137, 138, 139, 140, 142
Johnson, Susannah, 154
Johnson, Warren, 155, 158
Johnson, Sir William, 2, 5, 8, 9, 10, 11, 12, 13, 14, 15, 17, 18, 19, 20, 21, 22, 23, 24, 26, 27, 28, 29, 30, 31, 33, 35, 36, 39, 45, 46, 47, 48, 49, 50, 51, 57, 59, 60, 75, 80, 112, 138, 149, 159, 160, 161, 165, 174, 177, 178, 181, 199, 202, 203, 211, 222

238 Index

Johnson, William of Canajoharie, 11, 15, 20, 66, 75
Johnson, Sir William Gordon, 164
Johnson Castle, 23, 57
Johnson, Family Genealogy of, 161–164
Johnson Hall, 15, 21, 59, 60, 64, 65, 138, 145, 149, 161, 172, 177–181
Johnson, Mount, 10, 12, 23, 24, 57, 161, 178
Johnson, Old Fort, 10, 12, 13, 14, 16, 17, 18, 20, 21, 22, 23, 24, 25, 29, 66, 67, 68, 134, 145, 151, 158, 165, 166, 172, 174, 178, 199, 201
Johnson's Greens, 145, 146
Johnson's Settlement, 8, 10, 57
Johnstone, Rev. Mr., 74
Johnstone's Settlement, 72
Johnstown, 14, 15, 18, 48, 60, 64, 65, 66, 105, 131, 137, 138, 161, 174, 180, 181, 211, 231

K

Kaghneghtaga (Brant), 155
Kaiaghshota, 47
Karacanly, 120
Kayaderosseros Creek, 10, 136
Kayaderosseros Patent, 175, 177
Keder's, Riff, 112, 114
Killing of the Maidens, 81, 88
King, Charlotte, 22
King George, 22
Kingsborough, 64
Kingsborough Patent, 14, 152, 158, 174, 177
Kingsland or Royal Grant, 151, 154, 155, 158, 174
Kirkland, Rev. Samuel, 106, 211
Klock, George, 76
Klock, John, Jr., 64
Klock's Field, 111, 114
Knouts, Mary, 175

L

Lachine Rapids, 2,
Lafayette, Marquis de, 106
Lalande, 28
Lawyer & Zimmerman Patent, 156
Lebanon, Conn., 21
Lewis Family, 124
Lewis, Henry, 124

Lewis, Morgan, 116, 117
Liberty, Sons of, 127
Link, Matthias, 157
Lucknow, 58
Luzerne, Mountains, 28
Lyman, Fort, 30, 31, 32, 35, 36
Lyman, Gen. Phineas, 29, 30

M

McDonald, Donald, 131, 133
McGinnis, Captain, 36
McGrah, Christopher, 155
McGrah, Mary, 155
McKean, Capt. Robert, 114, 115, 116, 117, 118, 125, 126, 127
McKim, 22
McMaster, James. 64
Macdonnell, Capt. John, 122
Maddeson, Corporal, 88
Mahicans, 27, 28
Maxwell, George, 16
Meath, Ireland, 2
Mellon, Colonel, 89, 90, 95, 96, 97
Memoirs of an American Lady, 52
Meyers, Col. T. Bailey, 24
Michillimackinack, 40
Mohawk Legends, 189, 197
Mohawk River, 5, 8, 10, 11, 14, 23, 24, 45–57, 74, 82, 85, 86, 89, 92, 109, 120, 121, 124
Mohawk Valley, 28, 69, 71, 81, 85, 86, 105, 108, 111, 112, 130
Mohawks, 14, 20, 21, 27, 28, 30, 32, 33, 39, 45, 48, 50, 52, 66, 69, 70, 74, 78, 81, 105, 106
Monroe, Lieut. Col., 37
Montagnies, 27
Montcalm, Marquis de, 37
Montgomery, Gen. Richard, 128
Morris, Gouverneur, 127
Musquetoons, 25
Myers Family, 124

N

Niagara, 22, 46, 48, 49, 107, 119, 120, 138
Niagara, Fort, 59
Nose, 121, 124

O

Ogwagas, 14, 69, 70, 71, 72, 73, 74, 105, 109, 110
Old Fort Creek, 10, 24, 57

Index

Oneida Lake, 104, 107
Oneidas, 14, 45, 66, 70, 79, 80, 87, 89, 103, 105, 106, 107, 114, 117, 119, 120, 121
Onondaga Lake, 107, 118
Onondagas, 45, 70, 105, 106, 170
Oriskany, 21, 22, 61, 75, 79, 81, 84, 92, 95, 102, 106, 129, 144, 145, 180, 214, 221, 230
Ostrander, Lieut., 88
Oswego, 107, 111, 121
Oswego River, 107
Otsego Lake, 109
Ottawas, 39, 45, 50
Oudenarde, 6
Outram, Gen., 59

P

Painted Rocks, 201
Parkman, Francis, 29, 51
Pearson, Prof. Jonathan, 19
Perrian, Father, 28
Pesci Siro, 170
Phillips, Alexander, 8
Phillips, Hamilton, 8
Phillips, Lewis, 9
Plateau, James, 187
Plattsburg, 38
Pontiac, 14, 39, 40, 41, 42, 45, 48, 50, 51
Pool, a half-breed, 75
Pottawatomies, 45
Pownell, John, 8
Prevost, Lieut. Augustine, 156
Putnam, Miss Clara, 15, 16
Putnam, Dewitt C., 186
Putnam, Garrett, 186, 187
Putnam, Jan, 186
Putnam, Victor, 186

Q

Queen Anne's Chapel, 10, 77, 143, 198
Queen Esther, 110

R

Randall, Charlotte, 22
Randall, Henry, 22
Résumé of History of War of the Valley, 81
Richmond, A. G., 171
Rogers, Major, 39

Rome, 82, 84
Royal Greens, 68

S

Sacandaga, 143, 151, 174, 177, 233
Sammons, Frederick, 62
Sammons, Jacob, 62, 125
Sammons, Sampson, 62
Sanford, Hon. Stephen, 172
Saratoga, 105, 137
Schenectady, 8, 16, 85, 111, 135, 137, 200
Schoharie, 108, 111, 113, 120, 121, 143, 156, 227
Schoharie Creek, 182
Schoharie Indians, 70
Schuyler, Han Yost, 98, 100, 101, 102, 103, 104
Schuyler, Jeremiah, 16
Schuyler, Madame, 52
Schuyler, Nicholas, 101, 102
Schuyler, Col. Peter, 82
Schuyler, Gen. Philip, 66, 71, 74, 79, 83, 91, 129, 139
Scott, John Morin, 128
Schroon Lake, 143
Senecas, 45, 46, 48, 49, 50, 51, 105, 106
Sharon Springs, 123, 124
Shawnees, 42, 45, 46, 51
Shell Bush, 130
Shell, Christian, 130, 131, 132, 133
Shepard, Horace, 17
Shirley, Gov. William, 12
Shoemaker, 100
Simms, Jephtha R., 70, 75, 112, 147, 180
Singleton, Mr., 91
Small, Capt., 132
Smith, Geo., 16
Smithtown, 2, 161
Spencer, Thomas, 21, 75, 103, 106, 210, 211, 212, 222, 223
Stanley, Mildred, 203, 205, 206, 208, 209, 210, 211, 212, 215, 226
Stanley, Robert, 198, 199, 200, 203, 204, 209, 210, 211, 213
Stanley, Rudolph, 203, 204, 206, 207, 209, 212, 217, 224
Stanley, Therese, 203, 204, 209, 210, 212, 215, 217, 224
Stanwix, Gen. John, 82
Stevens, Arrent, 177
Stevenson, Capt. James, 159

Index

Stewart, Daisy, 226
St. François Xavier du Sault, 29
St. Leger, Lieut.-Col. Barry, 79, 8 , 84, 87, 92, 93, 98, 100–105, 145, 211, 212, 214, 221
Stockwell, Lieut., 93
Stone Arabia, 108, 111, 113, 114, 122, 130, 153
Stone, W. L., 8, 9, 62, 69, 71, 77, 106, 109, 114, 147
Stringer, Samuel, 159
Stuart, Rev. John, 77
Sullivan, Gen. John, 106, 107, 108, 110, 111, 122, 138
Summer Rambles, 182
Susquehanna River, 105, 109, 126
Susquehannocks, 45
Sutton, Samuel, 159, 160
Swartwout, Captain, 88

T

Tanner Family, 124
Teg-che-un-to, 11, 15, 20, 21, 75, 150, 151, 155, 204, 206, 210, 211, 212, 222 (William of Canajoharie)
Thompson, Captain, 121
Tice, Gilbert, 66, 90, 153, 159, 160
Ticonderoga, Fort, 31, 37, 38, 127
Tiononderoga, 198
Tracey, Gen. de, 28
Tribes Hill, 186, 189
Tryon County, 61, 63, 64, 73, 81, 83, 123, 137, 144, 146, 160, 172, 209
Tupper Lake, Big 67
Turnboul, Lieut. Alexander, 24, 26
Tuscaroras, 14, 105, 106

U

Unadilla, 73, 74, 75, 111

V

Vagaries of men's minds, 54
Van Rensselaer, Gen. Robert, 111, 113, 114, 115, 116, 118, 119, 122

Van Schaick, John, Jr., 16
Vaudreuil, M. de, 35
Vedder, Albert, 16
Veeder, John, 62

W

Wagner, Joseph, 75, 76
Wall pieces, 25, 26
Walrod, Hendrick, 120
Warren, Anna, 5
Warren, Lady, 7
Warren, Sir Peter, 2, 5, 6, 9, 161
Warrentown, 2
Washington, Gen. George, 160, 139
Watt, Robert, 167
Watts, John, 167
Watts, Hon. John, Jr., 169
Watts, Miss Mary (Polly), 16, 60, 145
Webb, Gen, 37, 82
Weisenburg, Catherine, 10, 19, 149, 161
Welch, Lieut., 88
Wemp, Jan, 198
Weston, Col., 89, 100
West Point, 128
Wheelock, Dr., 21, 211
White Mingo, 47
Whiting, Lieut.-Col., 33
Whitmore, Seth, 231
Willett, Edward, 127
Willett, Col. Marinus, 81, 87, 89, 91, 93, 96, 101, 123-129, 133, 197, 213, 220, 233
William Henry, Fort, 36, 37
Williams, Col. Ephraim, 33
Wilson & Abeel, 175
Wood Creek, 31, 82, 98, 99, 107, 209, 214, 217
Woodworth, Capt. Solomon, 130
Wyandots, 46, 47
Wyoming, 105

Y

Young, Almarin, 16

www.ingramcontent.com/pod-product-compliance
Lightning Source LLC
Chambersburg PA
CBHW070228230426
43664CB00014B/2239